T0087748

BELIEVING WOMEN IN ISLAM

Believing WOMEN IN *Islam*

★

A Brief Introduction

ASMA BARLAS
DAVID RAEBURN FINN

UNIVERSITY OF TEXAS PRESS AUSTIN

Copyright © 2019 by the University of Texas Press
All rights reserved
Printed in the United States of America
First edition, 2019
First reprint, 2020

Requests for permission to reproduce material
from this work should be sent to:
Permissions
University of Texas Press
P.O. Box 7819
Austin, TX 78713–7819
utpress.utexas.edu/rp-form

The paper used in this book meets the minimum requirements of
ANSI/NISO Z39.48–1992 (R1997) (Permanence of Paper). ♾

Library of Congress Cataloging-in-Publication Data

Names: Barlas, Asma, author. | Finn, David Raeburn, author.
Title: Believing women in Islam : a brief introduction /
Asma Barlas and David Raeburn Finn.
Description: First edition.
Austin : University of Texas Press, 2019.
Includes bibliographical references and index.
Identifiers: LCCN 2018023751
ISBN 978-1-4773-1588-0 (pbk. : alk. paper)
ISBN 978-1-4773-1589-7 (library e-book)
ISBN 978-1-4773-1590-3 (non-library e-book)
Subjects: LCSH: Women in the Qur'ān. | Women in Islam.
Women's rights—Religious aspects—Islam.
Qur'ān—Criticism, interpretation, etc.
Qur'ān—Theology.
Classification: LCC BP134.W6 B285 2018 | DDC 297.1/2283054—dc23
LC record available at https://lccn.loc.gov/2018023751

doi:10.7560/315880

CONTENTS

NOTES ON STYLE

Readers who search for scholarly notes and references will find them in short supply in this volume. Conventional academic studies quoting texts cite the title, its author, its publisher, the date and place of publication, and the page number(s). The digital age permits a healthy change of practice specifically for students of Islam. Accordingly, so far as possible, and in the interest of simplification, we have tried to reduce this academic practice in citations of translations of the Qur'ān. The website http://corpus.quran.com offers the works of seven major English translators together with Arabic recitation, original Arabic, grammatical analysis, and other useful information. References to verses of the Qur'ān in this text will provide just the verse number and the translator's surname; for example, "4:34 (trans. Ali)."

In some instances, English translations have been emended by David Raeburn Finn. Each emendation is noted, as are reasons for changes.

PREFACE

A Simpler *Believing Women*

ASMA BARLAS

This volume is an introduction to my book *Believing Women in Islam: Unreading Patriarchal Interpretations of the Qur'ān* (University of Texas Press, 2019), and it explains, in simple terms, how I read Islam's scripture and why. In brief, Muslims believe that the Qur'ān is God's word exactly as it was revealed to the Prophet Muhammad in seventh-century Arabia. Although most Muslims will point out, correctly, that the Qur'ān gave women certain inalienable rights 1,400 years ago, the truth is that for much of their history, most Muslims have interpreted the Qur'ān as privileging men. This is because, out of its 6,000 verses, five or so have been interpreted by some scholars as giving husbands certain nonreciprocal rights vis-à-vis their wives.

When I first read the Qur'ān in my teens, I stumbled over these so-called "hierarchy verses" because I found the rest of the text so uplifting. For instance, it teaches that God is beyond sex/gender, that God created men and women from the same Self, that both were made God's representatives on earth as well as one another's mutual custodians, and that God will judge them in light of the same standards. Given such teachings, I could not figure out why God would have given husbands greater rights than their wives in some areas. But at the time I knew nothing about interpreting texts.

Decades later I returned to this question, but by then I knew that Muslims had a long history of sexual discrimination and abuse, which they justified by drawing on one word in each of these five or so "hierarchy verses" (less than 0.01 percent of the text). By then

I also understood that what a text appears to be saying depends largely on who reads it, how, and in what sorts of historical and political contexts; in other words, there is a relationship between method and meaning. Beyond that, I had learned about hermeneutics, patriarchy, and Muslim religious and intellectual history. Rereading the Qur'ān in light of these new insights allowed me to see that, significantly, none of the "hierarchy verses" says that the reason God gave men certain rights is because they are biological males or because they are superior to women. At best, then, the verses addressed the prevailing conditions in seventh-century Arabia. Furthermore, the meanings of these verses change if we interpret some words differently, including the word that many Muslims interpret as "beat" (as in "wife-beating"). Like other languages, Arabic is rich and complex, and quite often a word can mean not only different things but also opposite things. Most of all, I came to understand that when we project theories of male privilege into the Qur'ān based on the assumption that men are made in God's image and God prefers them to women, we are denigrating the Qur'ān's depictions of God. In the Qur'ān's telling, God is one, uncreated, does not beget, is not begotten, and is incomparable since "there is none Like unto [God]" (112:4 [trans. Ali]). Minimally, then, God is not male, man, son, or father. This is why the Qur'ān forbids Muslims from calling God "Father" or even comparing God to anyone, meaning that its own allusions to God as "He" are simply a function of Arabic and not accurate depictions of God's being. Additionally, the Qur'ān urges Muslims to read the whole of the text (rather than piecemeal), to privilege its clear verses over the more metaphorical ones, and to search for "the best" in its meanings. This last injunction clearly suggests that not all the meanings we ascribe to the Qur'ān are necessarily the best, and also that our notions of what is "best" are liable to change over time.

To this end, I framed my own reading of the Qur'ān with its descriptions of God in mind and also applied a comprehensive definition of patriarchy to it, which readers of the text had not so far done. By *patriarchy* I mean both the tradition of rule by the father/husband and the contemporary claim that biological differences make men and women unequal. When I applied this definition to the Qur'ān, however, I could not find any teachings that support rule by the father/husband or theories of sexual differentiation, which is why I called it an egalitarian and anti-patriarchal text at a time when even some Muslim feminists were convinced that, at best, it is "neutral" toward patriarchy (Wadud 1999). Although this way of speaking about the Qur'ān is no longer uncommon, stereotypes still abound about its alleged patriarchalism.

This book, *Believing Women in Islam: A Brief Introduction*, covers a broad range of issues while excluding discussions of theology, methodology, and hermeneutics. Brevity was a goal. After all, it is meant to introduce readers to issues of patriarchy and sexual equality arising from interpretations of the Qur'ān before they proceed to the wider issues with which I deal more fully in the revised *Believing Women in Islam: Unreading Patriarchal Interpretations of the Qur'ān* (2019). Although I had contemplated writing a "simpler" version for many years, I never did get around to doing so. Consequently, when David Raeburn Finn, a Canadian philosopher with a burgeoning interest in Islam whom I did not know (and still have not met) offered to condense and simplify the book by adopting more user-friendly language, I took him up on his offer. What you have in your hands is the outcome of his diligent efforts. However, it is not a straightforward adaptation of my work, as we originally intended; rather, it is a product of remixing, by which I mean that while most of the arguments are from the book *Believing Women*, David also offers his own take on some verses and has added a new chapter (8) of his own as well as an afterword.

This volume includes eight chapters. Chapter 1 lays out, in plain English, the dispute between patriarchal and egalitarian readings of the Qur'ān with some examples. In addition, it provides a context for understanding that the Qur'ān's messages are framed in language that is susceptible to different understandings. Since God is just, all-merciful, and all-knowing, God's word (the Qur'ān) is not meant, and cannot be meant, simply for a localized contemporary humanity of the time of its revelation; it is instead meant for all humanity, for all times. Chapter 2 continues by noting some misogynistic pre-Islamic (or *jahiliyah*) practices regarding women. It points out that the Qur'ān's patriarchal exegesis ascribes male domination and discrimination against women to the Qur'ān, which implies that God either didn't notice or didn't care about the injustices involved in male privilege. To that end, chapter 2 provides examples of verses that explicitly reject inequalities.

Chapters 3 through 5 engage with patriarchal interpretations, revelation, Sharīʿah (divine law), and equality before the law, as well as with the Qur'ān's rejection of the imagery of God as male/father. These chapters simplify the corresponding chapters of *Believing Women*, while also making an additional argument (in chapter 5) about the roles that misleading gendered idioms (called "epicenes" in grammar) play in Abrahamic discourse about the divine.

Chapter 6 examines the Qur'ān's approach to equality and difference, taking as its themes sex and sexuality. It basically addresses the question of whether the Qur'ān supports a biologically based impairment of women's roles. It also offers additional material on verses 2:222–23 that undermine the patriarchal claims that husbands have the exclusive right to initiate sex and choose the sex act, and that their choices aren't subject to their wives' acceptance; that is, they are not mutual.

Chapter 7 focuses on patriarchal interpretations of women's public/marital/family rights and adds an interpretation, by Waqas Muhammad, of the so-called wife-beating verse (4:34), which many Muslims read as allowing a husband to strike a disobedient wife. The chapter subsection on "Adultery, Polygyny, and Disingenuity" disputes patriarchal readings of 2:282, which states that two women witnesses are required in a legal proceeding. David and I also offer divergent readings on the details of polygyny (marrying more than one wife) as conveyed in verse 4:1–6; however, both our readings contest patriarchal legitimizations of the idea that the Qur'ān permits generalized polygyny. The section on "Divorce and Misreading 2:228 for Male Privilege" provides a liberatory re-reading that demonstrates men's so-called advantage over women (*darajatun*) is not really an advantage.

Chapter 8, written by David, considers recent themes denying a liberating Qur'ān. These include the contentions that the Qur'ān most often addresses men on matters of sexuality, and that it contains unfailingly patriarchal verses. Further, these two facts suggest a sense of revelation-era equality that allowed for women's spiritual equality but also ordained a male-privileging pecking order. He provides egalitarian readings for each supposedly "unfailingly patriarchal" verse and shows that both Islamic history and the Qur'ān itself are consistent with a liberated Qur'ān: no notions of equality and justice alien to the era of revelation are needed for a liberating reading of the Word. Finally, in his afterword David traces how he, as a philosopher and student of Islam, came to be involved with *Believing Women*, complete with some academic teasing.

ACKNOWLEDGMENTS

We would like to thank our editors, Jim Burr and Sarah McGavick, and manuscript editor Amanda Frost at the University of Texas Press, as well as freelancer Alexis Mills for her copyediting and Lindsay Starr for the fabulous cover.

— I —

Interpreting Scripture

A Core Dispute

ISLAM, LIKE CHRISTIANITY AND JUDAISM, informs us of who we are, what God expects of us, and how we may meet those expectations. It advises us of imperfections that bar our salvation. Islam is home both to those who, on the one hand, read its sacred text, the Qur'ān, as teaching sexual inequality and the oppression of women, and those who, on the other, understand its teachings to be liberating for women.

The former view supports patriarchy in Islamic societies based on a conservative reading of the Qur'ān. We'll be more precise about patriarchy in Islam in due course, but by way of example, patriarchy makes the foundational claim that women are defective. Thus, a famous ancient Islamic scholar claimed that God spoke thus of Eve: "Were it not for . . . Eve the women of this world would not menstruate, and they would be intelligent and, when pregnant, give birth easily" (Muhammad ibn Jarir al-Tabari [b. 838, d. 923], *The Commentary on the Quran*, 280–81). If anyone mistakenly thinks that such claims have disappeared from the face of the earth, consider the following comments from a contemporary Saudi Arabian imam, scholar, and (at the time) religious advisor to the king:

> The Prophet Muhammad said about women: "I have not seen anyone more deficient in intelligence and religion than you." And, Islam . . . has shown that the twisted nature of women stems from their very creation. This is how God wanted woman to be. . . . Therefore, the husband should not make her do anything that is contrary to her nature and to the way she was created by God . . . he should turn a blind eye to her mistakes, he should tolerate her slips and errors, and put up with all the silly ignorant things she might say, because this constitutes part of the nature of her creation. (Saleh Al-Fawzan, Memri TV, clip no. 1, 483, June 11, 2007)

According to this view, women are sinful, stained by Eve's original sin, unclean, weak, lacking in intelligence, and therefore divinely ordained to be ruled by fathers and husbands.

Of course, patriarchies need not be misogynistic (women-hating), but the patriarchy illustrated in the above quotations is certainly so. To oppose such a view is to argue first that the Qur'ān doesn't support it. It's to show that the Qur'ān enjoins equality and warns against oppression based on gender without denying biological differences between men and women. Further, if conservative scholars and believers argue for an Islamic misogynist patriarchy, what evidence comes from the Qur'ān? What evidence comes from sources external to the Qur'ān?

NOTES ABOUT GOD, REVELATION, AND THE PROPHET

In the broadest sense, the dispute we approach is about God's message, about what it was. The message was first revealed to the Prophet, who reported it to his Companions and followers, who memorized each chapter (*surah*) and verse (*ayah*). The process of writing down the revealed Word began during the Prophet's lifetime.

Interpreting God's message wasn't always easy, but the Prophet explained as much as he could during his lifetime and provided a model for others in his deeds. Collectively, his words and deeds became the Prophet's Sunnah, or, to be precise, reports about the Prophet's words and deeds became his Sunnah. Those stories are called *ahadith* (sing. *hadith*). Understandably perhaps, some *ahadith* were made up or wildly inaccurate, and some were not.

"Allah" is the Arabic name for the God of Islam. The Arabic God is the same God as that of Christianity and Judaism. All three religions believe in a single God (that is, they're monotheistic). All three religions share the fundamental belief that God is all-powerful and the Creator of the Universe. As to why all three monotheisms have the same God, it's because if the Christian God were different from the Judaic God, and the latter were different from the Islamic God, then none would be all-powerful (because the others would be equally powerful). Secondly, if each of three distinct gods created "the" universe, there would be three universes. But the universe is everything, and there can't be three "everythings." So the Creator, God, is one. As we go along, we'll refer to the divine being simply as God.

The being who is God is referred to by many other descriptive names. Each name illuminates features of God's nature. It isn't easy to get a grip on God and God's capacities. God is all-knowing, most compassionate, most merciful, completely just. Understanding any of God's characteristics is a stretch. Nonetheless, we understand what we mean when we speak of ourselves, of our friends, and of others as being knowledgeable, of possessing compassion or a strong sense of justice, even of someone showing mercy. So we have some idea of what a being might be like who possessed immeasurable compassion.

We also come to grips with compassion by seeing what it is not. People who utterly lack compassion are rare. But they exist. God and God's capacities are important because of this most central dispute in how Muslims interpret God's word, the Qur'ān. If God is all-knowing, most compassionate, just, and merciful, then the Qur'ān's message isn't limited to a single age and a single group or people within humanity. If it were so limited, the Word would then ignore compassion, justice, and mercy for each and every believer of all eras, implying that God is less than all-compassionate and all-knowing. God foresees and understands all ages and all humanity.

The Prophet brought the word of God to the world. When he first married, he lived in Mecca. He often ascended a local hill and sat in the shade of a cave, contemplating. This is where he received revelation, God's messages. His initial confusion and fear gave way to acceptance. He was gifted with an extraordinary mind and a surpassing memory. Those who knew him before he ever became a prophet found his capacity for honest dealing and speaking the truth remarkable. He passed along God's word to those who would listen, just as God asked. God's messages became the Qur'ān.

What's written may differ from what is meant. How many times have you heard "You don't mean that" when you meant exactly that? God's word might mean many things, only some of which may be understood by the humanity of a given age or epoch. Other meanings, or applications or words or precepts, may be obscure to the humanity of a given age or era. The Word the Prophet brought was directed first toward the Arabs of the seventh century. But it wasn't meant simply for the local population, the humanity of that time and that place. God does not discriminate: humanity includes all humanity that is and will be.

DIFFICULTIES WITH WORDS

An all-knowing god would surely anticipate difficulties: people like nothing more than to argue about words, particularly written words. An all-knowing god would also anticipate that the difficulties would get worse because the Qur'ān would be translated from Arabic into every language of the world, giving rise to new arguments about whether the translated words captured the meaning of the original Arabic. If you thought those were the only difficulties, you'd be mistaken: some of the Qur'ān's verses are parables, lessons framed as allegorical stories. Some listeners might confuse the allegory meant as a moral lesson with historical fact. Some of the verses contain metaphors, and listeners may mistakenly take the metaphorical language literally.

Of course, the Prophet wasn't all-knowing. Even if he was extraordinary, he was simply a man, although a particularly good and noble one, chosen by God to receive the Message, "the Word," as believers say. But this simple man had friends and enemies. He knew from personal experience that words could be twisted, turned, and pummeled into shapes whose meanings were only dimly discerned by human readers and listeners. Early on he was reviled as a sorcerer, a magician, by some of his relatives and other people he knew. His followers were abused, tortured, ridiculed, and killed. But even some of his followers, perhaps most of them, were at times puzzled by the messages God transmitted through the Prophet. The society in which he received the Word was largely polytheistic (or pagan, as monotheists are inclined to say). Most people worshipped in front of stones believed to represent gods and goddesses. How could clarity be introduced to the Word? How could outsiders be brought to accept the faith? How could believers be brought to greater understanding of the Message?

HELPING TO UNDERSTAND THE WORD

God and the Prophet both tried to help, in different ways, with the anticipated difficulties that people would have understanding the Word. Perhaps most important is that readers of the Qur'ān are enjoined to read it as a whole so that comparisons between different verses and passages can be made for clarification. God instructed the Prophet thus:

> And say: "I am indeed one
> That warneth openly
> And without ambiguity
> (Of just such wrath)
> As We sent down
> On those who divided
> (Scripture into arbitrary parts),
> (So also on such)
> As have made [the] Qur'ān
> Into shreds (as they please)
> Therefore, by the Almighty [Rabb],
> We will, of a surety
> Call them to account,
> For all their deeds."
>
> 15:89–93 (TRANS. ALI)

Phrases, sentences, and passages were not to be taken out of context: that context is the whole Qur'ān. The most probable reading should be taken from comparisons of verses.

> Those who listen
> To the Word
> And follow
> The best (meaning) in it:

Those are the ones
Whom God has guided, and those
Are the ones endued
With understanding.
39:18 (TRANS. ALI)

The Prophet himself said to his daughter Fatima, who was puzzled by the Word, "I am the best *salaf* for you." Today we'd say, "I'm the best model for you." (The Arab word *salaf* literally means "predecessor.") He wasn't being immodest. He meant to help: if believers were confused about marriage, about prayers, about raising children, settling disputes, dealing with money, or other matters, they should follow the lead of someone chosen by God to receive the Word, a man who himself tried to understand and follow its best meaning, a man who, to the best of our knowledge, did exactly that. The Prophet's words and deeds are his Sunnah (an important Arabic word we'll speak further about below).

ARGUMENT: PATRIARCHY OR EQUALITY

Muslims in some countries reasoned like this: if the Qur'ān is patriarchal, does God not intend that we should reflect patriarchy in our laws and in our punishments for infractions of these laws? Shouldn't we have laws that reflect what God intended? Many women know these are not idle questions. Violence against women by husbands and family members exists in all countries. But in Muslim countries it is often justified by appeals to the Qur'ān and to the *sunnah* attributed to the Prophet.

For instance, in Pakistan, Hudood ordinances were enacted in 1979 purporting to be based on the Qur'ān and the Prophet's Sunnah. Women were raped, even gang raped, and reported the attacks to authorities. But they weren't able to prove the rapes because, according to misreadings of the Word, they were required to have four male witnesses. Consequently, women who reported being raped were sentenced for adultery. Thus, during the late twentieth and early twenty-first centuries, thousands of Pakistani women suffered rape, shaming, and incarceration, not to mention physical harm and unwanted pregnancies. In some Gulf monarchies today, notably Saudi Arabia, moral police roam public places targeting and beating women for immodesty. In some Muslim countries, women are deprived of education, forbidden to leave their homes without male guardians, required to veil in public, constrained from seeking medical treatment, and forbidden to drive. In some of these countries the obligation to honor the male head of the family is heightened to such a degree that any imagined slight against his honor by a female family member may call for her murder. In some such societies, female genital cutting, stoning, and sexual assaults are authorized based on conservative and patriarchal readings of the Qur'ān, even though there is no mention of such practices in the text itself.

Briefly then, some readings and interpretations of the Qur'ān's words are misogynistic in that they license oppression of women by men. Such practices include subordination, beatings, incarceration, and murder. Our questions are deceptively simple. How do misogynistic patriarchal readings square with the Qur'ān as the word of God? How do they square with our knowledge of the practice and conduct of the Prophet?

Notice something: these questions aren't about male domination as opposed to feminism, a century-old aspirational political movement demanding equal rights for women that emerged in the West. Rather, the core disagreement we're considering is about God's remedy, as transmitted through the Prophet, for the imperfect world of humanity. It's about whether the Qur'ān envisages equal rights for women and men or not.

The Qur'ān

God's Remedy for an Imperfect Humanity

WHY WOULD GOD be prompted to address the Word to the Prophet? It's unlikely God reckoned all was well in a world where people were given to the worship of stones, referred to in the Qur'ān as times of ignorance and idol worship. This pre-revelation period is referred to in Arabic as *jahiliyah*. Evidently their Creator knew that men and women are imperfect. But how did it get that bad? Even where the message that there is one God, the Creator, was promulgated (to the Jewish people by Moses, and to Christians by Jesus), people seemed to misunderstand or misinterpret details of God's message. Islam was meant to offer some clarifications.

In the period of *jahiliyah*, diverse communities of the Arabian Peninsula had different customs, languages, and styles of life. Women's rights varied from place to place. Their lives were not intolerable everywhere. In some areas women could become people of influence and wealth. In Mecca, notably, women were able to rise to high stations, act independently, and pursue a lifestyle where personal choice was both possible and welcomed.

Well before he was chosen to be the Prophet, Muhammad married one such woman, a wealthy and sophisticated businesswoman, the widow Khadija. It's often said she married him simply because of his honesty, an account that seems inconsistent with the complexity of human attraction. Khadija was the first to recognize what the Prophet's Companions and followers were later to understand: his intelligence, eloquence, and generous temperament endowed him with a compelling charisma. She admired him immediately and proposed marriage. A remarkable, open-hearted woman, Khadija regularly used her wealth to support orphans and widows. Their marriage lasted for twenty-five years, until her death, and the Prophet spoke of her for his remaining years.

In many other *jahili* communities, however, a man might have as many wives as he wanted and discard the "spares" as he chose. If he died, his wives were passed along without inheritance together with chickens, furniture, and other chattel to the deceased's eldest son, typically the son of another of the deceased's wives. Women were not permitted to eat some foods available to men, and no law forbade beating a so-called uppity wife with fists, rocks, bricks, or tools, even beating her to death. Women were given away in marriage without the right of consent. Some were married off after capture in war, sold in a slave market as "brides" whether they wanted to be married or not, and remained married only until the husband decided to divorce. Divorced women had no right to remarry. Female infanticide was common.

Women in *jahili* society were thus treated unequally, and the inequalities were of a kind that were clearly unjust. (Not all inequalities are unjust: a large man may consume more dinner than his tiny wife, yet both may consume what meets their respective needs.) If God recognized inequities in *jahili* society, injustices that afflicted women, what are we to make of those who claim the

Qur'ān supports a patriarchal supremacy, suggesting female inferiority and the inequitable treatment of women in religion, in marriage and divorce, in public and society?

There are just two possibilities here for those who claim that the Qur'ān supports a patriarchal supremacy in which unjust and inequitable practices continue to afflict women. God either (1) could not locate or (2) did not care about misogynistic practices in *jahili* societies. And don't think these stark alternatives are the end of the problem for patriarchal apologists. If God is all-knowing, God either knew and cared or failed to note or care about future generations. God's knowledge, which is complete, included an understanding of future social and economic development. In other words, God understood completely that our modern world would see; for example, violence against wives by husbands, lovers, and former lovers, and discrimination against women because they have monthly menses, become pregnant, and take time off work to look after sick children. Clearly God could not have failed to contemplate a future in which there are career women, single working mothers, women leaders of major countries, women scholars and professionals, police officers, physicians, scientists, engineers, truck drivers, and soldiers. Continuous economic and social changes may provide opportunities for new injustices, but also new remedies.

The question is worth asking: Would God, all-knowing and wholly compassionate, frame a message to future generations of men and women whose remedies were limited to misogynistic practices of seventh-century Arabia? Is the Qur'ān framed to forbid social and economic change? Are unjustly treated women of the twenty-first century thus obliged to revert to seventh-century practices of Arabia? Would such obligations to revert not themselves be unjust? For instance, conservative patriarchal readings of the Qur'ān suggest that if the practices of the twenty-first century cause injustice to women, the solution is to regress to practices of seventh-century Arabia. Thus, on a patriarchal reading, if today's woman is held back from promotion because of pregnancy, that's because she has no business working outside the home in the first place. On patriarchal premises, if an unveiled woman walking in a public park is sexually assaulted, it's because she should have been veiled; by walking in a public park unveiled, she has inflamed men with her sexuality, and she is to blame.

Alternatively, God might frame the Word to correct not only seventh-century imperfections but to anticipate those of later cultures and societies. If God offered remedy for the injustices of seventh-century *jahili* misogyny, was the Word not also meant to remedy misogynistic injustices of future centuries? The Qur'ān, in short, may incorporate deeper meanings that apply to the imperfections of future humanity. Here we locate the disagreement between patriarchal apologists and those who read the Qur'ān as a liberating text for women. The dilemma for patriarchal conservatives is this: If God recognized and offered remedy for seventh-century injustice but failed to recognize or ignored future injustices, either God is not all-knowing or, in the alternative, God lacks justice and compassion.

Back to seventh-century Arabia: Would an all-knowing God fail to notice murders of female infants? The beating and murder of wives? The treatment of wives as mere things attached to households in the manner of furniture, pots and pans, chickens, and pillows? Would a just and compassionate God fail to notice that within humanity, men's greater physical strength had led to cultural practices that subordinated and diminished those whose physical strength was not as great? Would God fail to notice that women's capacity to acknowledge and worship the Creator is not inferior to and, indeed, not in any way different from men's?

Whatever we think, what is clear is that God intervened in *jahili* Arabia: revelation came to an extraordinary man who visited a hillside cave near Mecca. God didn't ignore humanity's imperfections. Take, for example, the idea that women are inferior to men and cannot acknowledge and worship their Creator as men can. Here are some pertinent verses of the Qur'ān (all translated by Ali).

3:195 Their Lord responded to them: I never fail to reward any worker among you for any work you do, be you male or female. You are the issue of one another. . . .

4:124 Whoever as a believer acts righteously, man or woman, he or she shall enter Paradise and shall not suffer the least injustice.

33:35 God has promised forgiveness and great rewards to Muslim men and women, believing men and women, obedient men and women, truthful men and women, forbearing men and women, humble men and women, charitable men and women, fasting men and women who deny themselves, chaste men and women, men and women who are mindful of God.

Take the idea that female infanticide is permitted:

16:58–59 When a father learns his newborn is female, his face clouds over and he grieves. The bad news makes him hide from shame. Should he keep the child and be shamed or bury it in the sand? Certainly, his decision will be evil.

The message of this last verse isn't simply that the alternatives are both wrong; it's that a mind so blinded as to see shame or murder as its sole alternatives is already poisoned with evil. Moral character, which God rewards, requires dispensing with misogynist infanticidal traditions. God enjoins love and care for each and every child, regardless of sex.

Consider the Christian tradition that God created women as inferior beings, created them from Adam's rib (a bent rib, according to misogynists, all the better to show women's subservience to upright men):

7.189 God created you from a single being (*nafs*) and of the same being did God make his mate. . . . (trans. Ali)

The Arabic word *nafs* denotes a nongendered being from which both female and male were created, not Adam's rib. Or consider the idea that women are morally inferior, the original bearers of sin, because of Eve (referred to in Arabic as Hawwah, but who, it's worth mentioning, is not named in the Qur'ān):

> 7:23 They (Adam and his wife) said, "Our Lord we have wronged ourselves' souls. If you do not forgive us and bestow upon us Your Mercy we shall certainly be lost." (trans. Ali)

And,

> 20:121–22 Thus did Adam disobey his Lord, so he went Astray. Then his Lord chose him, and turned to him with forgiveness, and gave him guidance. (trans. Ali)

It wasn't just Adam's wife after all. They both listened to Satan (Iblis in Arabic) and ate the apples. Both were disobedient; both sinned. The Qur'ān provides no evidence that God sought to punish either Adam or his wife for disobedience, no evidence of the so-called Fall, and no evidence that Eve uniquely was to bear, not only for herself, but for all subsequent womankind, the curses of menses, painful childbirth, and inferior intellect.

REVELATION AND TWENTY-FIRST CENTURY PATRIARCHIES

The revealed Word clearly corrected and provided remedy for those who misunderstood Eve's role in what Christianity refers to as the Fall. Yet a twenty-first century spiritual advisor to the Saudi king accepts the idea that women are deficient in intelligence and religion, quoting the Prophet in support. This Saudi religious scholar illustrates a mystery. No words of the Qur'ān support his demeaning contentions concerning women. He must, then, if he is in some or other sense to be deemed rational, appeal to what purports to be evidence distinct from the word of God. But here we are presented with an even more profound puzzle. The Saudi scholar purports to quote the Prophet, but the quoted words contradict the Prophet's revealed Word. Since the Qur'ān is the word of God, and Muhammad was God's Prophet, the Saudi scholar appears to suggest that the Prophet didn't accept the Word as transmitted to him. In the alternative, the scholar's quotation of the Prophet is mistaken.

Since we don't question the Prophet's reliability as the Prophet of God's word, we are bound to look into the post-revelation history of Islam. What might plausibly explain what we understand to be the Saudi cleric's preposterous suggestion that the Prophet didn't accept the Word he was tasked by God to proclaim?

— 3 —

Patriarchal Readings of the Qur'ān

IN THE AFTERMATH of the Prophet's death in 632 AD, Muslims faced problems. The extraordinary man whose words, conduct, and character had been a model for believers, a model through which they might better understand the Word, was lost. He'd been chosen by God. His compassion, singular eloquence, and intelligence had illuminated God's message. Who would now serve to clarify the Word, to remind believers of God's message, and to carry it to those who did not yet believe?

Islam had spread like a wildfire through the Middle East. Within its jurisdiction it absorbed not just more *jahili* tribes, but also communities of Zoroastrians, Christians, and Jews. The Qur'ān's message ordained no forms of government, favored no type of political organization or rule, defined no set of easily applied laws. If peoples of different religions and races were to live together, what rules should be in place to settle disputes? What forms of governance would be acceptable and effective?

In the immediate aftermath of the Prophet's death, the capable and well-meaning men and women who were his followers, including his wives and Companions, initially did their best to substitute, often reluctantly realizing their recollections of the Prophet's words and deeds (his Sunnah) might be faulty. Worse, some of his Companions, notably his wife 'Ayesha (Aisha), quickly remarked on a tendency of some hangers-on to invent stories about the Prophet's words and deeds for purposes of their own. The Companions' memories of the Prophet's words and conduct also became a foundation of stories (*ahadith*) of his practices in word and deed (*sunnah*). Some Companions became caliphs or held other positions of authority among believers, positions previously occupied by God's Prophet. But none bore his moral authority, and Companions gave differing accounts of the same incidents in the Prophet's life. Accounts of his words and actions came too from many who knew him less well, accounts that bore scant relation to the Sunnah witnessed by his wives or Companions, and no relation to the Qur'ān's text.

While the words of the Qur'ān were fixed, their interpretation was not. Scholars gave explanations (*tafsir*) of the chapters (*surah*) and verses (*ayah*) of the Qur'ān, sometimes appealing to *ahadith* of doubtful validity for support. Some, the scholar al-Tabari for instance, could write, "The Qur'ān says" without noting that it was, in fact, only his opinion about how a verse might be interpreted. Slowly, almost unnoticed, the status once reserved for the Qur'ān was extended to *tafsir* that contained *ahadith* contradicting the Qur'ān. Wise and scholarly men and women, believers all, had done their best to develop the practice of critical reasoning (*itjihad*) to apply to conflicting *ahadith*. Who authored the *hadith* in question? If the author lived well after the Prophet's death, could the *hadith* nonetheless be traced to a Companion? Did the *hadith* contradict the Qur'ān? But as Islam's reach extended into the lands of different religions and cultures, adaptations of the *ahadith* flourished, including some that accommodated the punishment of stoning for adultery, the story of Eve's original sin, stories requiring veiling in the interests of women's purity, stories suggesting that obedience to rulers was required even if they were despotic thieves.

Recall that the *ahadith/sunnah* were of vital importance because, in the explanations (*tafsir*) of scholars, they clarified the Qur'ān's meaning. Once clarified, the Qur'ān provided a source for Sharīʿah, from which Muslims derived their rules of jurisprudence and law (*fiqh*), viewed as the essential nucleus of Islam. By Islam's second century the utility of critical reasoning (*itjihad*) as a decisive tool for investigation came to be doubted. A miracle was needed to straighten out the pile of *ahadith* purporting to represent the Prophet's Sunnah. The "miracle" came in the form of commentators on the law. Al Shafi, an influential scholar, poet, author, jurist, and sometime judge, was one of them. He was devoted to the memory of the Prophet and to Islam. He was both brilliant and, on evidence, impatient (a trait otherwise virtually unknown among men). Al Shafi decreed that consensus (*ijma*) was a source for Sharīʿah and for interpretation of the Qur'ān. If *ahadith* on which consensus (*ijma*) had been reached conflicted with the Qur'ān, the *ahadith* ruled. Notably, and with utter inconsistency, Al Shafi's decree itself didn't stem from consensus (*ijma*). It came instead, at best, from independent reasoning (*itjihad*). At worst, it arose because he'd run out of patience: he'd seen too much bickering and disagreement. His decree purported to be in the interest of protecting "religious knowledge." Rethinking (*bida*) was deemed innovation.

This whole process of reasoning may not have been so straightforward, but its consequences were. First, consensus was anointed, blessed, canonized, and set, if not in stone, certainly in tar; secondly, *tafsir* and *ahadith*, explanations and stories, were treated as possessing religious authority more fundamental than that of the Word. Privileging *tafsir* and *ahadith* meant privileging not the Qur'ān, but interpretations of it by perhaps a dozen men of Islam's second century. These men did not represent the ethnic, racial, or geographic diversity of Muslims at that time. Many of them were also immersed in a pre-revelatory misogyny originating in and perpetuating at least some of the deeply entrenched practices and understanding of *jahili* humanity. These few men's interpretations, not the holistic reading of the Qur'ān enjoined by its text, were then taken as the ultimate measure of the text's meaning. Scholars of Qur'ānic interpretation were henceforth relegated to the task of discussing traditionalists' explanations of the Qur'ān (*tafsir*). Being who they were, these scholars and intellectuals engaged in discussions of explanations that engendered further explanations and critical commentaries on earlier commentaries and explanations. And so on.

The Qur'ān disparaged nepotism in political rule but was otherwise silent on governance. Rulers within newly Islamic countries needed laws legitimizing their rule, however brutal or corrupt. Laws accommodating customary practices of Christians, Jews, Zoroastrians, and *jahili* subjects would make their rule less troubled. Increasingly, scholars and lawyers "discovered" *ahadith* conveniently incorporating both nonbelievers' and *jahili* pre-Qur'ānic cultural practices. Even more *ahadith* were "discovered" favoring obedience to rulers. Consensus validated these *ahadith,* even if at the expense of the Qur'ān's precepts. The long and the short of it is that the *ahadith* had been politicized. *Ahadith* of this period also absorbed Arab, Mediterranean, Judaic, and Christian cultural norms for women; they came to be seen as morally and religiously defective temptresses—unclean, unfaithful, and ungrateful toward their spouses. According to some *ahadith,* their intellectual inferiority made them unfit for politics. Reliable *ahadith*, those authenticated by scrupulous witnesses to the Prophet's words and actions, had been swamped by inauthentic, politicized companion *ahadith.* The swamp was both deep and murky.

The politicization of the *ahadith* permitted conservative Islamic scholars to glue God's word to the times of the Prophet. Believers and future converts were to model their lives on what were inaccurately, even grotesquely, portrayed as the practices of Arabia's seventh century, whether they were genuinely the Prophet's Sunnah or not. *Ahadith* could now be cited to justify nepotistic rule, beheadings, subjugation of women, and an interpretation of Islam in which the community of scholars did not include women because they were, after all, considered intellectually defective. A post-revelatory version of Islam, infected by doubtful *ahadith* and politics, grew naturally to support a male priestly class (imams, mullahs, and muftis) financially supported through an obligatory personal tax (*zakat* in Arabic).

The Qur'ān's holy word was understood through *tafsir*, the interpretations of clever men with no personal knowledge of the Prophet who, in their confusion and impatience, sought to end rational discussion by decreeing consensus of interpretations rather than revelation as the final arbiter of truth. Consider how this mattered on the notorious issue of veiling. Two sets of *ayat* (verses) informed conservative *tafsir* on veiling. In one set, the Prophet is instructed that believing women, including his wives and daughters, should wear a cloak [*jilbab*] when they go out (33:59–60 [trans. Pickthall]). In the second, believing men and women are both instructed to lower their gaze and guard their modesty. Further, women are counseled not to display their beauty and ornaments, "except what must ordinarily appear," and to "cover their bosoms with a shawl [*khumur*]" (24:30–31).

Conservatives read these verses not as counsel but as commands for believing women to veil because their appearance is otherwise sexually arousing. (Conservatives "knew" this, remember, because one *hadith* "proved" that Eve, that wanton woman, had convinced Adam to eat the apple.) But the so-called modesty verses are specifically addressed to the Prophet and are advisory, not compelling. They are counsel, not commands. Cloaks and shawls in that era covered bosoms and necks, not heads, faces, hands, or feet. Moreover, the counsel was designed specifically to differentiate believing women in Mecca from slaves and prostitutes at a time when *jahili* men commonly abused both. The *jilbab* marked believing women as off-limits.

The second set of verses invites both believing men and women to refrain from flaunting their sexuality, likely with the intent, again, of differentiating them from regular flaunters among *jahili* men and women. However, conservative readings of these verses interpret them as compelling women to veil to guard believing men from women's wantonness. The perversity lies, in part, in assuming that believing men possess the character of seventh-century *jahili* men. It lies further in the implication that an unveiled woman invites sexual abuse and, for the severe fundamentalist, may even deserve death in the name of Islam.

The Qur'ān, as read by conservatives, has a fixed religious meaning singularly addressed to seventh-century Arabia, even though conservatives, as do Muslims in general, recognize that its message is universal. Their misreading of veiling is a telling example. They confuse the Creator's speech with a command, though it is offered to the Prophet as counsel. Further, they confuse its audience (believing women in Mecca confronted with predatory *jahili* men) with all women. In locating seventh-century Arabia as the sole model (as paradigmatic), they are denying either God's knowledge of or compassion for all subsequent humanity; that is, they understand the Qur'ān to assert women's bodies are sufficiently wanton that women must veil to protect both men and themselves. Conservative readers of the Qur'ān default to an unwarranted insistence on *tafsir* (exegesis) based on consensus. Foundational conservative readings of the Qur'ān, *tafsir* of the second Islamic century, are based upon flawed *sunnah* reported in contrived *ahadith* formed to accommodate ruler politics and practices evidently conflicting with revealed Qur'ānic precepts. Sharīʿah, Islamic law, and the principles of jurisprudence (*usul al fiqh*) based on *tafsir* were corrupted by politically convenient and doubtful *ahadith*.

— 4 —

Methods and Revelation

Although their underlying principles are straightforward, a review and some explanations of the methods used in this book to interpret the Qur'ān may be helpful.

Islam grew from the word of God, who, the Qur'ān teaches, is uncreated, one and indivisible, and who may not be compared to others since "there is none" like God. Among other things this means, at a minimum, that God does not have a sex/gender and cannot be characterized as "she" or "he." This simple yet profound revelation challenges the common assumption that God is a male, an assumption made explicit in Abrahamic religions by almost universal references to God's commandments as "His" and to God as "the Father" and "King."

From the frequency of such references alone, many individuals easily proceed to identify earthly authority as the prerogative of men, for it seems to them that authority to rule is meant for them since they, not women, share God's sex/gender. Islamic monotheism corrects this view: the image of God as male/father/king is explicitly denied. Divine authority is neither male, nor is it shared. To put it differently, their biological sex does not give men any right to claim affinity with an unsexed/ungendered divine authority. Men cannot share God's sex/gender because God is without sex or gender. No support whatsoever for men's authority over women can be provided from the flawed understanding that God's authority implies a similar authority for one biological sex (male) over another (female). Indeed, the Qur'ān also does not define gender, such that one born as a biological male has certain character/gender attributes while one born a female has others. In brief, the Qur'ān does not say men, by virtue of being biological males, are intelligent, rational, and moral, and that women, by virtue of being biologically female, are unintelligent, irrational, and immoral. Yet this is what misogynists of all stripes everywhere claim.

What this conception of God means for readers of the Qur'ān is that since it is the word of God, no theologically sound understanding of the Qur'ān's teachings can proceed without first understanding the principles that God is without sex and gender, and that God's authority is indivisible and cannot be delegated to anyone. In fact, to try to partake in God's absolute unity and sovereignty by claiming to be sovereign over others is the only unpardonable sin (in Arabic, *shirk*) mentioned in the Qur'ān. Yet this is what Muslim men do in many societies today: they present themselves as earthly rulers over their wives in the assumed belief that being males/men, they are closer to God than women.

The God of Abrahamic religions is the Creator, all-knowing, just, and merciful. God does not deceive. The Word reflects God's justice and mercy, which are for all humankind. As for the man in question, long before Muhammad became the Prophet, he was celebrated for speaking the truth and for his scrupulous honesty. As we'll see, these basic tenets have consequences for patriarchal interpreters.

Earlier we noted that the Qur'ān came as a correction, a remedy for the injustices perpetrated by some people upon other people. (Remember, women were men's chattel, female babies were murdered. . . . You know the rest.) Men oppressed women. An all-knowing and perfect God can scarcely offer remedy for the injustices visited by men on women at one moment in humanity's history but ignore future injustices to future women throughout a constantly developing history. Such a speculation would mean God favored some women but not all women, that God favored some men but not all men. But God cannot be unaware of any injustice, and the Word cannot be thought to ignore them. The Qur'ān, in the broadest sense, addresses humanity's imperfections and thereby characterizes human perfection.

Texts may be read differently, but if readings are inconsistent with God's perfection, they fail a fundamental test of legitimacy. The Qur'ān contains both plainspoken text, clear and unambiguous, and passages relying on metaphor. As noted earlier, the plain and unambiguous language of the Qur'ān counsels that the text must be read as a whole, a method referred to by scholars as a holistic reading. To sharpen the message, the Word warns against selecting this or that passage to read without reference to others. The Book also counsels us to take the "best meaning" from the more ambiguous metaphorical passages.

Taking the best meaning from the Qur'ān's verses can't help but bring up questions about justice. Patriarchal interpretations of the Qur'ān suggest God's justice is consistent with men being the exclusive breadwinners, with men beating women, with women being denied an equal role in managing a family's affairs, with men having the right to decide on the when and how of married sex.

An observation or two is in order here because justice is a complex topic. Early in our experience as children we begin to learn about justice. Perhaps a sibling plays with our favorite toy without giving us equal time, or they're favored in some way we're not.

"It's not fair," we say. We learn that fairness is connected to justice: if something is unfair, it's unjust. Establishing fair practice establishes just practice (and a more peaceful household). Broadly, just practices establish equality: equal time with the toy, equal favor for each. But fairness is different from equality. An older sibling is bigger, so he might drink more milk because he needs to. Needs can sometimes affect what's fair.

Now think about justice in history. Some traditional readers of the Qur'ān believe it permits beating alienated wives, that it gives husbands that right. They believe the word of God permits men, not women, the right to decide on the when and how of marital sex. When egalitarians (those who read the Word as teaching equality, equity, and justice) suggest such practices are unjust, traditional interpreters argue that egalitarians are imposing a modern justice, one foreign to the era of the Word's revelation. Notice why traditionalists can't very well agree that this modern justice, which bans men from beating their wives and ruling the bedroom, is real justice at all. They can't agree for a very good reason.

Our understanding of justice is not static: it grows through history because in different societies and cultures, through different eras, different injustices afflict us. To make a long story short, our sense of justice is constantly illuminated, informed, and shaped by injustices we recognize and correct. By eliminating injustice, we realize justice. (Well, more or less. Sometimes what we think will eliminate an injustice may create a new one.) But if modern justice were real justice (or at least closer to the Book's counsel), and if it banned wife-beating and men-first-and-foremost, revelation-era justice would in practice be defective precisely because it permitted unjust practices. This is why traditionalists claim there is only one real justice: "It's fixed, frozen; it can't be changed. It's good old revelation-era justice. Women-know-your-place justice!" So traditionalists are stuck: they have to show their reading alone is supported by the Word. To put it another way, they must show there's no other way to read the Book.

If readings of patriarchal scholars incorporate counsels of injustice, then readings more consistent with justice are more consistent with the Word. Liberatory and egalitarian readings recognize that the difference between modern justice and revelatory justice is that the former improves the latter. Modern justice isn't an alien imposition upon an exclusive revelation-only justice; it is justice that has recognized and eliminated more injustices. Another way to put this is that, unsurprisingly, God's word is for all people for all times. How could it not be?

To summarize: in *Believing Women* Asma Barlas first defines patriarchy. Since patriarchal claims to male privilege/superiority may stem from association with God envisaged as possessing gender (for example, "His" commands, God as "King," God as "Father"), Barlas severs the connection by citing Qur'ānic counsel that God is without gender. Further, she adduces the Qur'ān's counsel that it must not be read piecemeal, but as a whole. Moreover, it must be read for the best meaning. Her aims in *Believing Women* are to show that the Qur'ān supports neither the tradition of father/husband rule nor male biological superiority.

— 5 —

Patriarchy

Patriarch (noun): 1. The father and ruler of a family; one who governs by paternal right.

IMPERIAL DICTIONARY OF THE ENGLISH LANGUAGE (LONDON: GRESHAM, 1900)

A GOD WITHOUT GENDER VERSUS GOD THE FATHER

CHRISTIANITY AND JUDAISM ASSERT, as does Islam, that there is one God, but Islam has a specific view of how God is to be represented. The Qur'ān declares:

Say: [God] is God
The One and Only
God, Eternal, Absolute.
God begetteth not
Nor is begotten.
And there is none
Like unto God.

SURAH 112 (TRANS. ALI)

So God is indivisible ("the One and Only"), incomparable, and unrepresentable ("there is none like unto God"). God's supremacy (sovereignty) is shared neither with other gods nor with humans ("God begetteth not"). God is neither a literal nor figurative father to humanity.

Jews and Christians
Say: "We are sons
Of God, and His beloved."

. . .

No, you are simply people,
Of the humanity God has created.
5:18 (TRANS. ALI)[1]

God's divinity and sovereignty cannot be divided: God is neither one divinity nor one sovereign *among others*. No genetic or spiritual patches of God's divinity are disbursed to humanity, still less on fathers/sons/men in contrast to mothers/daughters/women. The only unpardonable sin mentioned in the Qur'ān, as noted in the last chapter, is *shirk*, the extension of God's sovereignty to others. If God isn't Father, no earthly father can represent his own rule as based on a divine patriarchy (rule by the father/male privilege). To conceive of God as in any fashion human is to anthropomorphize (render human) the divine. To understand God's qualities as male (just, severe in judgment, stern) and/or female (compassionate, loving, nurturing) is simply to engender where gender does not apply.

PATRIARCHY AND THE SEDUCTION OF PRONOUNS

A secular twenty-first century feminist conference might well begin: "God has brought us together. She has done good work." This greeting would no longer be met by laughter, as it certainly would have been in the mid-twentieth century. But references to God as

"She" make the same error as do references to God as "He." Abrahamic monotheistic histories, including Islam's, write and speak of God as "He," of humanity as "His children." Of course, to render what is unseen understandable, we use language. What language could be used for our creator? The truth is all monotheisms face the problem of how to refer to God. Specifically, the problem is which pronouns are best suited to the task. "It" doesn't work: "It = God" transcends our understanding, alienating the divine from our experience. Humanity's experience is located in a world of things, of stuff. We are earthbound. We use *it* to refer to an animal, vegetable, or minerals, not to our image of God. If we celebrate and worship God, what is it we worship and celebrate? We are easily stumped, unable even to approximate what "It" could be. So how do we refer to God? If "It" is a non-starter, would "He" or "She" do?

Gendered pronouns attach figuratively to all manner of discourse where they become entrenched, persisting as virtual idioms. Ships, for instance, are resolutely feminine. "She's a well-crafted schooner/cutter/sloop." So are countries. Britain is the motherland of democracies; "God Bless America" contains the lyric "Stand beside her, and guide her. . . ." Russia too is the Motherland, and, just to be different, Germany is the Fatherland.

In Islam, Judaism, and Christianity, God became "He," "the Father," and humanity "His children." The gendered pronoun "He" comforts as "It" could not: it seems to nod toward something familiar. Quite possibly it appeals to a presumptive and deeply embedded patriarchal sensibility preexisting all monotheistic prophets. But "He" in reference to God is a gendered pronoun in appearance only. If we say "Man is doomed unless he reckons better with his environment," the words "man," "he," and "his" are known in grammar as epicenes, no more gendered than ships or countries. It should be acknowledged that many people, especially women, are alienated by this apparent gendering of humanity, even if it reflects merely an ancient idiom founded in ignorance. Yet despite such understandable alienation, most English speakers would accept that "Man is doomed unless he reckons better with his environment" pretty much comes to "Humanity is doomed unless it reckons better with its environment." Epicenes are understood as gender neutral even if we bristle at the flavor of their intimated gendering.

Epicenes pervade Abrahamic representations of God, giving rise to patriarchal illusions. Daily Jewish liturgy includes the beautiful *Avinu Malkeinu*, "God is Father and King." But to infer from the entrenched (epicene) idioms referring to God as "He" that God is male/father/king is akin to inferring that a "whale of a man" must be a whale. The Qur'ān, however, insists on God's incomparability. This precludes engendering God, specifically attributing a male humanity to God, whatever entrenched idioms are used to refer to the Divinity.

VICE-REGENCY AND PATRIARCHY

God appoints humankind as *khalifah*, vice-regents on Earth (2:30), on which, however, they are not to walk "with insolence" (17:37 [trans. Ali]). Similarly, those who "seek glory and power" are warned: "To God belongs All glory and power" (35:10 [trans. Ali]). Some patriarchal apologists suggest that since God is King, Lord, and Ruler, and they themselves are God's vice-regents, men have dominion over women. Further, by self-serving interpretation, some approve of wives prostrating themselves before their husbands. But first, of course, vice-regency is entrusted to *insan* (humanity), not simply to men. Secondly, men and women, who are equal vice-regents, don't inherit through their office a slice of divinity which might command prayerful prostration. Finally, God's sovereignty is indivisible, so in fact no part of it devolves to men or women.

ABRAHAM AND FATHERHOOD

Patriarchal apologists sometimes elevate and sanctify fathers/men because they misunderstand Abraham's role. The Qur'ān clarifies his story and significance at length. When Abraham set out to seek God, he misidentified first the stars, then the moon, and finally the sun as the Creator. In short order he recognized that each of them is transient, mere manifestations of God's power. Through his quest he experiences a revelation:

For me, I have set
My face, firmly and truly
Toward [God] Who created
The heavens and the earth
And never shall I give
Partners to God.
6:79 (TRANS. ALI)

But Abraham's father is a polytheist, and Abraham duly confronts his father's authority:

. . .
Oh my father! why
Worship that which heareth not
And see'th not, and can
Profit thee nothing?
Oh father, to me
Hath come knowledge which
Hath not reached thee:
So follow me: I will guide
Thee to a Way that
Is even and straight.
19:42–43 (TRANS. ALI)

Eventually Abraham destroyed the polytheists' idols, but failed in calling his father to Islam. He was saved from the fire (intended for him by his father and fellow polytheists) by God's mercy. For Abraham, God's rule trumped that of fathers.

Does the Qur'ān's Abraham story merely contrast unbelieving fathers with believing fathers? Is the point that unbelieving fathers are unworthy, not to be respected, but believing fathers' familial sovereignty is legitimized by association with God's sovereignty? No, this is not what the Qur'ān suggests. First, Abraham's submission to God's will made him subject to God's sovereignty, not an associate sovereign. Further, when God cloaks Abraham and his line with prophethood, it's as imams (religious leaders and models), not as fathers/rulers. Moreover, when Abraham, in a vision, agreed to God's request to sacrifice his son, he surrendered his rights as father to God's rule. Finally, Abraham gained his son's assent (without which the sacrifice would not carry moral weight) to subject himself to God's will, a pointed rejection of the traditional patriarchal rights of life and death a father held over his sons. It's vital to note that the Qur'ānic lessons of Abraham's story apply regardless of sex and gender; that is, disobedience to males/fathers is legitimized by faith, the faith of both women and men. Father-rule over children and women, seen as a counterpart sovereignty to God's, is an impediment to faith.

THE MAN WHO WAS THE PROPHET

At its core, the Qur'ān abjures patriarchal pretensions in favor of God's sovereignty. *Jahili* polytheists resisted the Word because it was foreign to "the ways . . . we found our fathers following" (5:104 [trans. Ali]). But the Qur'ān both targets polytheism and rejects vain insistence on male supremacy found among believers: Christians and Jews "take their priests And their anchorites to be Their lords in derogation of God. . . . Yet they were commanded To worship but One God" (9:31 [trans. Ali]).

The Prophet himself was, in fact, a father. When the question of his adopted son arose, the answer was: "Muhammad is not The father of any Of your men, but is the Apostle of God, And the Final Prophet" (33:40 [trans. Ali]). The Qur'ān thus reduces to naught the relative importance of fatherhood when weighed against the office of *imam* and Prophet. The Prophet's life and the Word he proclaimed have been subjected to a tragic irony by patriarchal apologists. Certainly, as we have seen, many of the *ahadith* narrating his purported Sunnah are falsely attributed. Worse, the *ahadith* reporting his Sunnah are permitted to abrogate the Qur'ān's teaching only because they purport to be his practice. So, in spite of the Prophet's extraordinary humility, a modesty that forbade his sanctification, his purported conduct as interpreted by conservative *tafsir* achieves an authority greater than that which he repeatedly recognized as supreme, the word of God. Far from sanctifying the Prophet's fatherhood, the Qur'ān even denies his precedence over his family and his people: "Thou art One to admonish. Thou art not One to manage [peoples'] affairs" (88:21–22 [trans. Ali]).

Although the Prophet asked his wives to be discreet and to dress modestly (to differentiate them from the indiscreet and immodest), he acknowledged their rights of free movement and treated them as intellectual and spiritual equals. After his death his wives refused attempts to restrict their movements, citing the Prophet's refusal to do so. Interestingly, some patriarchal traditionalists' attempts to sanctify the Prophet as man/ruler of his household have provided fodder for Islam's critics, who focus on the age of his youngest wife, 'Ayesha, and the fact that he had several wives. As far as 'Ayesha's age is concerned, the first biography of her life was written well over a hundred years after her death, and by that time she had become a polarizing figure in Muslim history for various reasons.[2] As such, even the earliest accounts of her life are already open to dispute. As for the Prophet's many wives, polygyny was a pre-Islamic practice, and some notable prophets, including King David, are said to have had nine hundred wives and concubines. In other words, conventions have differed for different prophets and at different times. In the Prophet's case, with the exception of 'Ayesha, his wives were widows or divorcees, beginning with Khadija[3] and Sawda bint Zam'a. Some needed protection for themselves and their children, such as a roof over their heads, while others had been widowed in war and were unable to provide for themselves and their children. Multiple marriages required by office and enjoined by the Prophet's sense of charity and his generosity of spirit are diminished by men who say they wish to follow his example (by marrying multiple women) but who forget that for twenty-five years of his life he was married to one woman, Khadija, who was not only twice-widowed but also fifteen years older.

In sum, the Qur'ān came as a remedy for patriarchal societies infected with misogyny. The Word speaks against engendering God with fatherhood and equally against investing fatherhood with a sanctity differing from that of motherhood. The prophets and interpreters of the Qur'ān are to be followed just insofar as they subject themselves to divine truth, and not because of their lineage or deemed interpretive expertise (see 9.31, 3:79–80).

— 6 —

Equality and Difference

Equal (noun): one not inferior or superior to another.
Equal (verb, transitive): to make equal, . . . to cause
to be commensurate with or unsurpassed by. . . .

IMPERIAL DICTIONARY OF THE ENGLISH LANGUAGE (LONDON: GRESHAM, 1900)

SEX AND SEXUALITY

THE PERPETUATION OF patriarchal supremacy both within the *umma* (the community of believers) and, specifically, among the *ulema* (Islamic religious scholars) requires the subordination of women. The appearance of a rational basis for such subordination depends upon locating defects in women; that is, a consensus of "evidence" must be adduced from the *ahadith*, from the *sunnah*, or from the Qur'ān to show that on the basis of sex one gender fails to possess those qualities which could, for instance, support political, social, commercial, familial, and scholarly equality. In brief, patriarchy presupposes that biological differences entail social impairment. Does the Qur'ān support a biologically based impairment of women's roles?

THE QUR'ĀN: EQUALITY AND DIFFERENCE

The Qur'ān's creation narrative differs from that of other Abrahamic faiths in that it says that a woman and man, co-created and equal, were brought into being as a pair from a single Self (*nafs*):

It is God
Who created
You from a single person [*nafs*]
And created its mate of like nature in order
That he might dwell with her (in love).
7:189 (TRANS. ALI)

None of the Qur'ān's thirty-odd passages dealing with humanity's creation report that man was created before woman or that woman was created "out of" man. Secondly, the Qur'ān does not single out Adam's wife as the initiator of disobedience to God, instead informing us that both Adam and his wife disobeyed God (7.23, 20.121–22). Finally, given that Adam's wife (Eve/Hawwah) was not singled out for disobedience, she cannot have been solely responsible for the Fall. There is, for instance, no Qur'ānic counterpart to God's damnation of Eve in Genesis (3:16). What's more, the Fall doesn't appear in the Qur'ān. Instead the pair's expulsion from Paradise permits a common humanity to proceed, a humanity which through faith and action subject to God's mercy may be worthy of salvation.

CARE, ACTION, AND FAITH

The Qur'ān obliges men and women to honor faith and its commands.

To believe in God
And the Last Day
And the Angels
And the Book
And the Prophets;
To spend of your substance,
Out of love for [God],
For your kin,
For orphans,
For the needy,
For the wayfarer,
For those who ask,
And for the ransom of slaves;
To be steadfast in prayer,
And practice regular charity;
To fulfil the contracts
Which ye have made;
And to be firm and patient,
In pain (or suffering)
And adversity,
And throughout
All periods of panic.
Such are the people
Of truth, the God fearing.
2:177 (TRANS. ALI)

Equally, the Qur'ān prohibits:

Shameful deeds, whether open
Or secret; sins and trespasses
Against truth or reason; assigning
Of partners to God, for which

[God] hath given no authority;
And saying things about God
Of which ye have no knowledge.
7:33 (TRANS. ALI)

Here the Qur'ān commands faith in moral practice and recognizes no gendered barriers to faith or practice. Insofar as patriarchal *tafsir* permits women's moral equivalency while simultaneously suggesting a biological impediment to their practice, the *tafsir* has no Qur'ānic basis. Men and women are equally capable of acting out of care for God's word.

For Muslim men and women,
For believing men and women,
For devout men and women,
For true men and women,
For men and women who are
Patient and constant, for men
And women who humble themselves,
For men and women who give
In charity, for men and women
Who fast (and deny themselves).
For men and women who
Guard their chastity, and
For men and women who
Engage much in God's praise
For them has God prepared
Forgiveness and great reward.
33:35 (TRANS. ALI)

Differences in sex in the Qur'ān do not entail inequalities, nor do they imply hierarchy or precedence.

O humankind! We created
You from a single pair
Of a male and a female
And made you into
Nations and tribes, that
Ye may know each other
(Not that you may despise
Each other.) Truly
The most honoured of you
In the sight of God
Is ([the one] who is) the most
Righteous of you.
49:13 (TRANS. ALI)[1]

God might have made a single people, but God's plan was to test humankind (see 5:51). Regardless of differences such as language, race, and religion that divide humanity, the test is to find and submit to God's will (5:51). Gender differences do not entail inequality.

The believers, men
And women, are caretakers [*awliya'*]
One of another: they enjoin
What is just, and forbid
What is evil: they observe
Regular prayers, practise
Regular charity, and obey
God and [God's] Apostle. . . .
9:71 (TRANS. ALI)

As caretakers of one another, men and women are enjoined to advise and counsel each other equally, without adversity, in the absence of references to precedence or hierarchy. Notwithstanding the Qur'ān's recognition of women's and men's equal rights and responsibilities in the sight of God, patriarchal apologists insist that some Qur'ānic verses treat women and men differently in the law, marriage, and divorce. We shall take specific patriarchal arguments up in due course.

THE RELIGIONS OF ABRAHAM AND SEXUAL EQUALITY

In order to understand what is specific about the Qur'ān's approach to sex and sexuality, it is useful to compare it with traditions from the other Abrahamic religions. For instance, Jewish traditions refer to menstruating women as *niddah* (impure and unclean) and require their separation for seven days, followed by five to seven days of chastity and ablutions to ensure all traces of menstruation are gone. Intercourse with a *niddah* is forbidden; even indirect contact with the *niddah*, such as touching her bed or sitting in her chair, makes one unclean, a condition alleviated by washing one's clothes and bathing. In a related but different vein, Christian traditions include the notions of purity achieved though permanent sexual abstinence (celibacy), the celebration of abstinence and virginity as marks of virtue, and the institution of prostitution as an outlet for a presumed bestial male sexuality. Islam, however, recognizes sexual desire as serving both individual instincts (pleasure) on the one hand, and God's will (the perpetuation of human communities) on the other.

QUR'ĀNIC SEX/SEXUALITY

> . . . [God] created from yourselves mates that you might find serenity [*sukun*] in them, and [God] ordained between you love [*mawaddah*] and mercy. Verily, in that are signs for those who reflect. (30:21 [trans. Ali])[2]

The Qur'ān here centers sexual/marital bonds in the serenity derived from the fulfilment of sexual intimacy. That fulfilment envisages mutual desire and gratification. Notably, it doesn't insist on sex solely and exclusively for procreation's sake. Equally, the Qur'ān neither contrasts sexuality with spirituality nor associates it with humanity's animal nature or corporality. Still less does the Word suggest that sex represents a human weakness. Rather, it recognizes mutual male/female desire and the shared serenity of desire's gratification. Men and women may be pure or impure, and the pure are to marry their own, and likewise the impure (see 24:26.) So purity and chastity are not ascribed solely to women, nor is either identified solely with abstinence or virginity. Chastity is located for both sexes in the avoidance of lust, lewdness, fornication, and adultery (see 24:3, 5:6). Chastity and purity may or may not be characterized by virginity, and virgins can be of either sex. Conduct, specifically in moral and sexual choice, defines chastity, not class, religion, or identity.

> Marry those among you
> Who are single, or
> The virtuous among
> Your slaves, male or female.
>
> 24:32 (TRANS. ALI)

Slavery, acknowledged by the Qur'ān, differs radically from the racist enslavement of "inferior" peoples that was practiced historically by white Europeans and the slave owners of the American South:

> . . . Ye proceed from one another; so wed [slave girls and concubines] . . . and give unto them their portions in kindness, they being chaste, not debauched nor of loose conduct. (4:25 [trans. Ali])

Thus the Qur'ān doesn't promote slavery. Instead it acknowledges the institution's existence within the society into which its message had been delivered. In 4:25, for example, female slaves are recognized as moral agents capable of chastity within marriage, and specifically capable of denying sexual predation. Elsewhere in the Qur'ān, the notion of manumission (freeing of slaves) is introduced as an atonement for sins.

SEX, THE VEIL, AND THE GAZE

The Qur'ān introduces two concepts of veiling, one associated with eyes (the gaze), the second with clothing. God instructs the Prophet to inform:

> Say to believers that they should lower their gaze and guard their modesty. . . .
>
> And say to the believing women that they should lower their gaze and guard their modesty . . . [and] not display their beauty and ornaments except what (must ordinarily) appear . . . [T]hey should draw their veils over their bosoms and not reveal their beauty. (24:30–31 [trans. Ali])[3]

Traditional patriarchy suggests women are to be segregated and veiled to protect men's virtue. But 24:30–31 directly undermines this traditional interpretation. First, the instruction to wear shawls (*khumur*) and lower their gaze assumes women's presence in public places. Secondly, instructions on casting down one's eyes are imparted to both men and women. Traditional patriarchal notions of segregation and veiling are an evident corruption of these counsels. While it's the gaze that effects the veil, both men and women are to dress modestly (specifically, to cover private parts). However, Muslim traditionalists have tortured 24:30's message to extract an instruction to cover women's faces and hair, requirements never mentioned in the Qur'ān. Furthermore, traditionalists ignore explicit instructions about male immodesty in changing clothes (see 24:58), the import of which is to require men to disrobe in private.

Doubtless the body, as the Qur'ān describes it, is both sexed and potentially erotic, an eroticism moderated by appropriately modest dress in public and a sense of propriety with respect to disrobing. The Qur'ān's counsel of modesty nowhere implies that the body is sinful or unclean. Rather, since the body and its bearing may promote desire, the careful attention of all who possess bodies is warranted.

As an aside, modern discourtesies may be noted. Many Western commentators, including feminists, disparage Islam, seeing the *niqab*, *chador*, and even the *hijab* as evidence of Islam's universal oppression of women. It's true that some Muslim countries, even more particularly some Muslim subcultures, require forms of dress unwarranted by Qur'ānic counsel. On the other hand, it's also true that some Muslim women choose their garments for modesty, perhaps having found that, worldwide, some men are prone to unwelcome, even predatory behavior. Those in Western countries who see the *niqab* as invariably a mark of oppression of women or, alternatively, as a calculated affront to local Western customs of dress miss its role as a personal choice for modesty.

PATRIARCHY: WOMEN AS PROPERTY

Traditional patriarchy locates two *ayat* (verses) to warrant the claim that wives becomes their husbands' possessions. Let's treat them one by one.

> Fair in the eyes of men is the love of things they covet: women and sons; heaped up hoards of gold and silver; horses branded (for blood and excellence); and (wealth of) cattle and well-tilled land. Such are the possessions of this world's life; but . . . nearness to God is . . . best. . . . (3:14 [trans. Ali])

Patriarchal apologists mistakenly read 3:14 as a license to covet women. Far from identifying women as property, the verse merely contrasts men's worldly desires with more enduring spiritual goals. It neither equates women with property nor suggests that a love of women is an impediment to closeness to God.

The second *ayah* is close to the heart of misogynist patriarchy. With the introduction of Islam, a new religion of Abraham, men of a previously *jahili* society appear to have been unsure as to how and when sex might be initiated in and around menstruation. How were they to treat their wives during menses? *Ayat* 2:222–23 instruct the Prophet how to deal with such questions:

> . . . Say: it is an annoyance [*adan*]. So leave women alone at such times and do not seek their intimacy until they bathe. After they have bathed, then seek intimacy as God has enjoined. Truly God loves those who turn to God, and loves those who care about cleanliness. Your women are a garden [*harth*] for you, so visit your garden as you wish. . . . (2:222–23 [trans. Ali; emended by Finn])[4]

Note that this *ayah* addresses men and offers them guidance couched in metaphorical, not literal, language. In the translation above, we use the phrase "seek intimacy" while Ali's Arabic paraphrases speak of "going to," as in "go to your home." Translators of Arabic to English versions have followed patriarchal *tafsir* in translating *harth*, proposing "a place of sowing of seed," "place of cultivation," "tilth," "fields," and "tillage." These translations certainly accord with one *literal* Arabic reference for *harth*. That said, it's worth asking whether any of them reflect the metaphor intended in the Qur'ānic language. First, *harth* meaning "tilth" is an inappropriate metaphor where *harth* is a feature of Paradise.

To any that desires
The [*harth*] of the Hereafter
We give increase
In his [*harth*]; and to any
That desires [merely] the [*harth*]
Of this world, We grant
Somewhat thereof, but he
Has no share or lot
In the Hereafter.
42:20 (TRANS. ALI)

"Tilth" was already archaic in mid-twentieth century English and invariably referred to prepared agricultural soil in earlier usage. But if we read the *harth* of 2:222–23 and that of 42:20 as having the same import, "tilth" makes little sense. Traditional English translations of *harth* in 42:20 vary from "rewards" to "harvest." Again, "harvest" does accord with an early Arabic *literal* translation of *harth*. But if we wish to locate an English counterpart with both an agricultural/sexual import and connotations of the blessings of Paradise—that is, a single common noun capturing both the potential fecundity alluded to in 2:222–23 and agricultural connotations of the Hereafter's rewards (*harth*) in 42:20—the closest English word would be "garden." Gardens offer the enjoyment of both fruits and flora, of beauty and bounty. Gardens are places of repose and offer sustenance for body and soul. They invariably respond to and reward those who tend to them: they are alive. "Garden" makes seamless sense of the metaphorical use of *harth* in both Qur'ānic *ayat*.

(It's true that the Qur'ān elsewhere uses the Arabic *jannat* specifically to refer to the Gardens of Paradise (see 47:15), but that scarcely precludes use of the metaphor suggested by *harth* to conjoin conceptual imagery of men's love for women with the counterpart rewards of the Hereafter.)

Traditional patriarchal understanding of *harth* as "tilth" in

2:222–23 suggests the passivity of seedable soil, thus supporting the idea that wives are a form of inanimate property, passively subject to men's sexual desires. But *harth* of the Hereafter (42:20), if it is to be consistent with Qur'ānic Paradise, must connote a flourishing abundance, eternally gratifying, eternally pure, serene, bathed in harmony and compassion. Translating *harth* in 42:20 as "harvest" suggests abundance, but also the abundance of something harvested, already cropped, no longer growing, itself passively available for consumption. Moreover, "harvest" suggests the proximity of decay, the finality of growth and mordant excess. In short, understanding *harth* as "harvest" provides a picture inconsistent with Qur'ānic Paradise. But if the language in 2:222–23 is metaphorical, which it is, the appropriate metaphor for men "seeking intimacy" would be men seeking to enter a garden, namely that of their wives' sexual intimacy. The *harth* of 42:20 cannot represent a static collection of cropped edibles because Paradise offers an infinitely flourishing and rewarding garden. The symbolism of each *ayah* suggests a living garden, a picture of love and sexuality consistent both with Qur'ānic love (2:222–23) and with the eternal garden of the Hereafter (42:20).

Furthermore, menstruation in the Qur'ān (2:222–23) is treated as an inconvenience, a trial. Together with other biological functions common to humanity, it invites bathing in its aftermath. Neither the menstruating woman nor menstrual blood is singled out as polluting, as they both are in the two other Abrahamic traditions. So menstruating women are permitted to pray in mosques and to participate in Haj. One can therefore read 2:222–23 as "go unto" (or "approach") one's wife in the aftermath of menstruation, with desired intimacy understood as a husband and wife tending to each other, mutually cultivating the garden of their intimacy. This translation captures the vibrant richness suggested by the *harth* metaphor understood as a garden, whereas the agricultural "tilth" and "harvest" do not.

However, the Qur'ān's patriarchal exegesis of 2:222–23 centers on the phrase "visit your garden as you wish" to suggest not only that the initiation of sexual intimacy is solely at the discretion of the man but also that the type of sexual act is for the man to choose (whether or not his wife agrees). Thus three claims are made: (1) the man alone has the right to initiate sex; (2) the man chooses the sex act; and (3) his choices are not subject to his wife's acceptance—that is, they are not mutual. In fact, all three claims are inconsistent with the text.

Recall who is addressed in 2:222–23, and why. God invites the Prophet to address men because men may suffer confusion about menstruation and permissible intimacy. Part of believers' confusion may well have arisen because of Jewish traditions of menstruation as an impurity and the associated ritual chastity of some duration, traditions that would have been well known in seventh-century Arabia. A natural questions for men of the day was: Are we, believers in Islam, to follow those traditions?

The question to which 2:222–23 is addressed is therefore: "When may we seek our (menstruating) wives' intimacy?" The sense of the answer given is to provide the following advice: "Stay away *during* her menses, but *after*, *once* she has bathed, *then*, bearing in mind what God has enjoined on these matters, go to her as you wish." So, to return to the first claim, consider the assertion that "man alone has the right to initiate sex":

1. 2:222–23 advises men not about a *right to sex*, but about *when* sexual activity is permitted: "keep away *during* their courses," "do not approach them *until* . . .," "*after* they have cleansed," "*then* go to them." The *ayah* does not give men the right to initiate sex with their wives. (Still less does it restrict the initiation of sexual intimacy, or the seeking of sexual intimacy, to men.) Instead, it answers the question to which the *ayah* is a response: "When may men, with God's blessing, seek intimacy with their (recently) menstruating

wives?" Hence, while the *ayah* informs *when* he may seek intimacy, it does not say the wife may not seek intimacy.

Secondly, as to the man choosing the sex act:

2. The right to seek a wife's intimacy is distinct from the right to a wife's intimacy. Further, no part of seeking a wife's intimacy "as (that is, *when* [*anna*]) you wish" ("as you like" or "when you like") provides support for the man's right to choose to have sex since the adverbial phrase is temporal in application. The husband may not "go to" ("approach") her during her menses. Instead, he may "go to" her "as" (that is, "when" [*anna*]) "he wishes" ("not during her courses," "not until . . . after she bathes," "then seek . . ."). No part of "as he wishes" or "when he wishes" suggests he has a right to choose to have sex, let alone to do so without her consent.

As to the final issue of the husband's unilateral right to choose how he acts:

3. No torturing of the wording of 2:223 may extract the meaning of a man acting "however he wishes," still less "however he wishes" without regard to what his wife wishes. In any case, to translate *anna* ("as") in an utterly temporal context as "however" is a simple and obvious mistranslation.

In sum, the Qur'ān clearly acknowledges biological sexual differences. Fertile women, after all, are subject to menses. The Qur'ān invites men to note this inconvenience to the extent that they forbear seeking intimacy with their partner until this inconvenience has been dealt with. The *ayat* 2:222–23 embody a counsel of graceful courtesy for men and the wisdom of love's patience. Thus, they provide no evidence whatsoever for the precedence or superiority of men's rights based on sexual differences.

— 7 —

Family, Marriage, and Equality

CONSERVATIVE PATRIARCHAL *tafsir* limits women's rights in the public sphere. They are unsuited for public office, according to conservatives, because they are intellectually deficient as an enduring consequence of Eve's alleged sin in the Garden of Eden. This misogynist view, as already noted, conveniently ignores the fact that Eve is not mentioned by name in the Qur'ān, is noted only as Adam's wife, and is jointly responsible with Adam for disobeying God. As an aside, this instance of patriarchal *tafsir* presents a remarkable challenge for genetic scientists, a challenge not simply because such an intellectual deficiency has been undetectable historically, but also because if such a deficiency were passed to women from the Ur-mother Eve, how it avoided being passed on equally to the male issue of the same mother would present a considerable genetic mystery.

But misogynist Qur'ānic interpretation doesn't limit itself to women's public roles. It's equally inclined to confine women's rights in those most intimate of human institutions, marriage and the family of that marriage. Within disparate Muslim cultures, misogynist interpretations have regrettably led to the empowerment of husbands as owners of a wife and children, with rights to abuse, even murder, family members. Does the Qur'ān support such interpretations? Does it support a husband's ownership of his wife and children? Does it support the submission of his family members to him or his right to abuse his wife? Does it support male privilege and precedence?

MARRIAGE, FAMILY, RIGHTS, AND RESPONSIBILITIES

Islamic marriage is contractual, thus in the legal, public, and social realms. But the conduct of married partners within marriage is prescribed in the practice of faith. The Qur'ān also addresses the rights of children by informing us of the responsibilities of the father: he is responsible (provided he is the breadwinner) for providing economically for his wife and children, including his daughters, even if they are divorced. No parental rights are peculiar to fathers. The reciprocal obligations of children are those of respect and kindness, particularly toward aging parents:

> . . . be kind
> To parents. Whether one
> Or both . . . attain
> Old age in thy life.
>
> . . .
>
> . . . address them
> In terms of honour.
> And, out of kindness,
> Lower to them the wing
> Of humility, and say:
> My Creator, bestow on them
> Thy Mercy even as they
> Cherished me in childhood.
>
> 17.23–24 (TRANS. ALI)

God commands children to honor not only fathers, but both parents, who together have cherished rather than ruled them as infants. Each of us is enjoined to care for our parents—in particular, mothers, who first bear children in swells of pain and then wean them over two years (see 31.14). But gratitude to one's parents has its limits:

> . . . Show gratitude
> To Me and to thy parents:
> To Me is thy final Goal.
>
> But if they strive
> To make thee join
> In worship with Me
> Things of which thou hast
> No knowledge, obey them not;
> Yet bear them company,
> In this life with justice
> And consideration. . . .
>
> 31.14–15 (TRANS. ALI)

Three points are made here. First, parents are not intermediaries between God and children. Secondly, all children are to come to God's truth as individual moral agents independent of and, if necessary, even in conflict with the views of their parents. Finally, even if children are expected to disobey erring parents, they are simultaneously reminded to care for and be fair to them.

REVERING GOD AND MOTHERS

The Qur'ān invites humanity's reverence both for the Creator and for the mothers who bore them in their wombs:

O humanity: revere
Your Creator,
Who created you
From a Single being [*nafs*]

. . .

Show reverence for God, through Whom
You demand your rights,
And reverence the wombs
That bore you: for God
Ever watches over you.

4:1 (TRANS. ALI)

Comparing reverence [*taqwa*] for God to that for mothers clearly does not suggest parity of reverence. It insists that believers recognize and venerate God the All Merciful [*Rahman*], God the Creator [*Rahim*]. Equally it insists that believers venerate the wombs [*rahim*] that "bore them," thus grounding the believers' understanding of God's infinite capacities in the familiar nurturing tenderness and compassion of women/mothers. The Qur'ān thus privileges mothers over fathers, to whom it never extends the concept of reverence [*taqwa*]. So whereas patriarchal misogynists may sentimentalize references to motherhood, the Qur'ān insists on the righteousness of reverence for mothers.

MARRIAGE, SAMENESS, EQUALITY

Islamic marriages are legal contracts. This contract essentially transformed the pre-prophetic status of a *jahili* wife as chattel to that of a woman with legal status, capable of enforcing legally binding marital rights. Prenuptial terms of the contract might reject polygyny and define the wife's rights to a divorce, a divorce settlement, and child custody. This assumption in the Qur'ān of a woman's right to contractual marital security directly implies that sexual equality is prior to marital rights; that is, equal marital rights are a consequence of the equality of the sexes, not the other way around. Recall that men and women originate in the same Self (*nafs*), they "proceed from one another" (Qur'ān 2:195). An even clearer assertion of sexual equality is found in another verse:

God has made for you
Mates and companions of your own nature
And made for you, out of them,
Sons and daughters and grandchildren. . . .
16:72 (TRANS. ALI)

Qur'ānic rules of marriage also ordain fulfilment in love between partners who care for one another, and mercy between them (see 30:21). Even where religious difference or enmity come between couples, the Qur'ān enshrines forbearance, forgiveness, and compassion (see 64:14, 64:2, 4:19). If sexual equality and compassion characterize Qur'ānic marriage, patriarchal misogynists nonetheless argue for a contrary position, one which claims to find verses (*ayat)* ordaining male marital privilege and even wife-beating. One such famous verse, often seen as the ultimate weapon of the misogynist patriarchal armory, has been translated as follows:

Men are protectors
And maintainers of women,
Because God has given
The one more (strength)
Than the other, and because
They support them
From their means.
Therefore the righteous women
Are devoutly obedient, and guard
In their husband's absence
What God would have them guard.
As to those women

On whose part ye fear
Disloyalty and ill-conduct
Admonish them first,
Then, refuse to share their beds,
Lastly, beat them (lightly);
But if they return to obedience,
Seek not against them
Means of annoyance.
4:34 (TRANS. ALI)

Ali's translation inserts the word "strength" even though there is no Arabic counterpart. But his translation correctly recognizes men as "maintainers" of (breadwinners for) women. Many Arabic-English versions mistranslate the key word, *qawwamun*, then use that to explicitly claim that the verse asserts male privilege: "Men are in charge of women," "Men are protectors," "Men are the managers of the affairs of women," "Men are superior to [women]." Both "maintainers" and "breadwinners" are by all accounts warranted by the Arabic meaning of the word *qawwamun*. Male privilege, however, is neither suggested nor implied. So how was that conclusion reached?

MARRIAGE AND DIVORCE IN THE QUR'ĀN: WAQAS MUHAMMAD

Yusuf Ali is not alone in providing mistranslations; for example, adding "strength" without textual warrant for Qur'ān 4:34. Further, his reading of *qawwamun* to privilege men, a common traditionalist misunderstanding, is not his sole mistake, nor the worst he makes. Happily, an alternative exists: Waqas Muhammad, who represents himself modestly as an amateur researcher, has provided scrupulous scholarship with remarkable conclusions on the issue of the so-called wife-beating traditional *tafsir* found in 4:34. His *tafsir*[1] locates 4:34 in the broad context of marriage and divorce.

The proximate context (in the form of the two immediately preceding *ayat*) is wealth and inheritance, followed by kindness and giving.

> And do not envy what God bestowed with it, some of you over others. For the men is a portion of what they gained, and for the women is a portion of what they gained. And ask God from his favour, God is knowledgeable over all things. (4:32 [25])

> And for each We have made inheritors from what the parents and the relatives left, and those you made an oath with you shall give them their portion. God is a witness over all things. (4:33 [25])

Muhammad painstakingly dismantles patriarchal understandings of each relevant phrase of the immediately subsequent 4:34. Patriarchal translations mistakenly suggest that men "excel" women and are "preferred" by God. He argues effectively for the following translation of the verse's beginning sentence:

> . . . men are maintainers of the women with what God bestowed on some of them over others and with what they spent of their money. (4.34 [82])

What then of the patriarchal contention that men are thus privileged, superior, and so the rightful managers of women's affairs? Here it is useful to recall that the Qur'ān was introduced into a misogynistic *jahiliyah,* the male component of which must certainly have questioned its newly prescribed roles according to God's word. If the Word provided remedies for *jahili* injustices, did those remedies extend into marriage and family? Men, whose world was changing, naturally had questions: "Are we still to be the maintainers, breadwinners, for our wives and families?"

Muhammad's argument (25–28) for this reading comes to this: when and if men spend their inheritance or earnings on the upkeep of their family (that is, when they provide for the family), they are maintainers of their wives and families. Thus the first sentence of 4:34 defines conditions under which men are maintainers of their wives and families. Note that such a definition doesn't imply that women/wives aren't, or can't be, maintainers of (breadwinners for) their spouses or families. Clearly, no all-knowing God, no God who contemplated all humanity of the present and future, could fail to contemplate a future in which breadwinners for a family might be of either sex. Consider: if a woman inherited more, or earned more, or earned when her husband didn't and spent her earnings or inheritance, she would satisfy the definition; she would, in fact, be the maintainer of her husband and family. Clearly, on the same basis, husband and wife may simultaneously be the maintainers of each other and their families. Further, each spouse individually, through different periods of employment and unemployment, might alternatively be and then not be a maintainer of spouse and family. Moreover, if a spouse is unfortunately widowed, the remaining adult, man or woman, is the family's maintainer.

As an aside (one of some importance), it cannot have escaped God's notice, nor would it have escaped that of the Prophet, that throughout the final marriage of her life, Khadija's wealth provided not only for her spouse and family but also for many of the earliest believers. Only two conditions must be satisfied for someone to be a maintainer of a family or a spouse: (a) to have money and (b) spend it on spouse/family. The designation "maintainer of family/spouse" is not gender-specific. To put the point in somewhat more modern terms, breadwinner is a job description rather than a gendered role.

If one begins with the patriarchal confusion that "men are preferred by God," as some translations of 4:34 begin, that they are the "managers of women's affairs," it might seem to follow that wives should be grateful, that they should express their gratitude by a duty-bound obedience to their husbands. So we find a common patriarchal translation as follows:

> Men are in charge of women by right of what God has given . . . So righteous women are devoutly obedient. . . . (4:34 [trans. Sahih International])

Other translations offer "Therefore righteous women are devoutly obedient"; and "the good women are therefore obedient." These translations mistakenly suggest, without explicitly saying, that the Qur'ān enshrines women's obedience (*qanit*) to their husbands presumably out of a sense of duty or gratitude because men are the breadwinners and preferred by God. Waqas Muhammad, like Amina Wadud, dispels this misreading by noting that the Qur'ānic *qanit* invariably expresses obedience to God or to God and his Prophet (28), not to men/husbands. His recognition of *qanit* as invariably connected to obedience to God illuminates the next part of the verse:

> . . . so the righteous women are dutiful, guardians to the unseen with what God guarded. . . . as for those women you fear their disloyalty, then: (first) you shall advise them . . . (4.34 [28])[2]

As Muhammad notes, the Arabic *takhafoona*, translated as "you fear," is in the imperfect tense, indicating not that one fears the affection of one's wife has been alienated, but that one is apprehensive she might be tempted in that direction (28). In turn, the husband's fear suggests he may not wish for the marriage's end, hence the introduction of counseling (25).

Muhammad also provides insight into 4:34 by comparing it with 4:128–30, where the shoe is on the other foot, that is, where a wife fears her husband's misconduct.

> And if a woman feared her husband's ill conduct or desertion then they bear no sin if they reconcile. Reconciliation is better. Souls are swayed by greed. But if you fear God, God is all-knowing. (4.128)
>
> Never could you deal equitably between women even if you desired. But be not disposed wholly to turn your back on her, so as to leave her without resolution, hanging. And if, fearing God, you reconcile, then God is all-Forgiving, all Merciful. (4.129)
>
> And if they separate, each will be enriched by God from His abundance. . . . (4.130)[3]

In 4:128–30, the wife's fear is expressed in the past tense. Something has happened, and he may desert her. The Qur'ān enjoins him not to leave her without resolution; in other words, not to leave her "hanging." Reconciliation is preferable, but divorce is the alternative. To leave one's spouse *without resolution* causes harm and requires the intervention of an authority (see 58:1–4). Conventional patriarchy, as we have seen from Ali's translation, reads 4:34 to mean that if one fears one's wife's affections may be alienated, one is first to counsel her, then abandon her in the marital bed (cease having sex with her).

The third step, according to Ali's conventional and patriarchal reading of *idriboo*, is that one is "to beat" her. Muhammad notes that in modern Arabic, *idriboo* can be a transitive verb, meaning it takes a direct object. So translators resorting to modern Arabic have little difficulty reading the tripartite series of actions in 4:34 to mean "advise her, shun her, *beat her*." But the Qur'ān did not emerge in the era of modern Arabic. It arose in an era of usage reflected only in the earliest dictionaries, from the era of classical Arabic. Muhammad's rejection of *idriboo* as "wife-beating" begins by noting that the word is derived from the root verb *DRB* (*daraba*), and he shows the following:

1. DRB occurs nowhere in the Qur'ān with the plausible meaning of "beat" (1–24).
2. Where DRB occurs with a direct object and without a prepositional phrase, it never means "beat" or "strike."
3. Where a body part, such as a hand, is mentioned as what to DRB with or body parts are mentioned as the objects that are DRB'd, there is no clear meaning of physically hitting or striking.
4. In its use as a transitive verb—that is, with a direct object—it invariably means "to put forth, cite, or indicate."
5. When used to mean "beat" or "strike," it requires the preposition "with" (*bi*) (58).
6. Further, and finally, no classical Arabic dictionary lists "beat" or "strike" for DRB except for the specific meaning of "to strike" where the prepositional phrase "with a weapon/in battle" is omitted by ellipsis (75).

Muhammad also reviews classical Arabic versus current usage, context, and internal consistency, and compares verses specifically related to marriage and divorce. His analysis undermines any plausibility for the contention that 4.34 instructs, permits, or enjoins a husband to beat, strike, or scourge his wife. He observes that 4:35 envisages the involvement of an authority and, further, that a procedure is defined for divorce or reconciliation (one judge from the husband's family, another from the wife's) [38]. But Muhammad suggests that the "authority" is likely to be involved only if it has been required or invited to be (38–39). After a prolonged "abandonment of her in the marital bed," the only resolution is to reconcile or divorce (2:226–27 [41]), a step that requires an authority.

Note the implications of the sentence immediately following the sequence "advise, abandon, *idriboo*": "Then if they respond to you, do not seek a way against them."[4] One implication is that some time has elapsed after counseling her and then abandoning her in the marital bed. The sense of the conditional sentence is that if some healing has occurred, then reconciliation is possible; that is, one's fear of the wife's alienation should not persist. But in the alternative, if healing has not occurred, if one continues to fear that she is no longer attached to the marriage, one is "left hanging." In this case the husband's marriage is *unresolved*, as is that of the corresponding wife in 4:128 and the "disputant" wife in 58:1–4. Where a spouse is left "hanging," the Qur'ān's remedy is to involve an authority. That is done by submitting facts to the authority to begin the resolution (see 58:1–4).

If 4:34 is read to mean that after counseling and shunning, the next step is to *idriboo* (beat) the wife, it suggests an important inconsistency. For the husband who "fears" for his marriage would thereby give her grounds for divorce (4:128). In other words, traditional interpretations have 4:34 offering steps to save a marriage that include a final step of beating, acknowledged legal grounds for divorce (Muhammad, 73).

Is there a meaning for *idriboo* consistent with the Qur'ān's known procedures for reconciliation and divorce? Muhammad notes that a primary and common meaning for *idriboo* in the era of the Qur'ān's emergence was "to cite" (42). (This use continues in modern English legal parlance. A police officer may cite a motorist for speeding. Technically, the police officer provides information about the motorist's speed and the posted limits on the respective road. The citation is then to be acted on by the courts.) Here is Muhammad's reading of 4:34 and 4:35 in full:

> The men are maintainers of the women with what God bestowed on some of them over others and with what they spent of their money, so the righteous women are dutiful; guardians to the unseen with what God guarded. And as for those women you fear their disloyalty, then: (first) you shall advise them, and (second) abandon them in the bed, and (lastly) cite them to the

> authority. If they obeyed you, then seek not against them a way; Truly, God is High, Great. (4:34)
>
> And if you (authority) feared a rift between them two, then appoint a judge from his family and a judge from hers. If they both want to reconcile, then God will bring agreement between them. God is Knowledgeable, Expert. (4.35 [82])

Waqas Muhammad's scholarship and argument are compelling, not least because "citing" the recalcitrant wife to an authority is precisely mirrored in the Prophet's role in dealing with a husband's reluctance to get on with either reconciling with his wife or giving her a divorce (58:1–4). (We'll return to 4:34 when discussing current patriarchal resistance to the notion that the Qur'ān supports liberation of and equality for women.)

ADULTERY, POLYGYNY, AND DISINGENUITY

Traditional patriarchal understanding devalues women's evidence in legal matters on the basis of *ayah* 2:282, in which a debtor is advised that his indebtedness and its terms of repayment should be recorded and witnessed either by two men or one man and two women (so that "if one woman forgets, the second may remind her"). Patriarchal understanding of this verse would extend the two-for-one rule to all legal matters, including civil and criminal testimony.

However, the claim that the Qur'ān warrants a two-for-one extension to all legal matters based on the debt contract example cannot be sustained. Ironically, it is belied even by traditional narration—namely, that of a young woman's sole testimony that a man attempted her murder, testimony accepted and acted on by the Prophet. It is belied by the historical fact that Naila bint al-Farafsa's sole witness testimony founded the campaign by ‘Ayesha and other

Companions to avenge the assassination of her husband, Caliph Usman. It is also belied by the fact that nowhere else but in 2.282, in the total of eight occurrences in which evidence and law are discussed, is two-for-one countenanced (4:6, 4:15, 5:106, 5:107, 24:4, 24:6, 65:2). Finally, it is belied by the fact that in respect of evidence in the case of adultery, one woman's testimony is accepted over that of the man (24:6–9).

It is also relevant to note that if a man accuses his wife of adultery, the word of God requires four believing men of good character to assert that they have witnessed the act (4:15). Thus 4:15 raises delicate questions about some men's capacity for dependable testimony. Why else require four honest men to substantiate an accusation? The fact that an accused woman's testimony is decisive against her husband's may suggest a divine understanding of the reliability of men as witnesses, on the one hand, and women's on the other.

For millennia, women believers have resisted citing 24:6–9 by way of noting that women are more reliable witnesses than men. Alas, a comparable courtesy has escaped misogynist practice. But if God has taken the measure of gender tendencies in witness reliability, what contingencies could reasonably explain 2.282's suggestion that two women might replace one man as a witness to a debtor's written contract? Why, in other words, does 2:282 provide an apparent exception to testimonial equality before the law? One possible explanation is that in the era of revelation, women were rarely literate and thus unable to recognize the inscription of their names, let alone write them. Even more rarely were women involved in commerce. We might imagine a debtor's contract presented years after its inscription to an illiterate witness, whether a woman or a man.

Q. "Is this your name?"
A. "I don't know." (The witness is unable to recognize the writing.)

Q. "Did you witness this document?"
A. "I'm not sure." (The witness may not recall doing so.)
Q. "Did the debtor agree to the following terms of repayment to the debt owner?"
A. "I'm not certain." (She may not recall precise details.)

The word of God recognizes and privileges women in acting as witnesses with the right to seek advice from another woman who, jointly with them, witnessed a document. Thus the Qur'ān acknowledges a cultural inequity, not a gendered one, based on differences in familiarity with written debt contracts, an inequity specifically located in the transformative era of the revelation. Given that specific cultural era, an unlettered woman's recollection of what she witnessed, particularly the exact details, might be more easily prompted by a question such as the following:

Q. "Do you remember this woman, also a witness to the contract?"
A. "Yes. I remember Maryam." (She may well remember her sister witness and so, through her, the event and its particulars.)

Note that 2:282 begins with the acknowledgement that the signatory debtor may well be a man of limited understanding; in a word, dim-witted and/or illiterate. It is consistent with 2:282, perhaps even likely, that such a debtor might select from among his friends an equally deficient male witness. The *ayah* clearly offers guidance for the protection of the debtor, who is reasonably seen as relatively disadvantaged since the grantor of the debt dictates the terms of repayment. Left unsaid, but intimated, is a further possibility: the dim/illiterate debtor and/or his potentially equally deficient male friend may need protective correction or guidance from one or both women witnesses. We noted above the Qur'ān's stand on the relative reliability of men and women as witnesses (24:6–9). Without suggesting for a moment that dull men, or indeed any man, ever dismissed a woman's observations simply because they were a woman's, God's wisdom in 2:282 permits a context in which men of potentially imperfect understanding, and male witnesses of possibly imperfect reliability, may be protected by calling on one or another woman as a witness, or both women together. After all, assumed illiteracy and commercial naïveté in the era of revelation should not have impeded women's good, perhaps even impeccable, recall and/or thorough comprehension of details forgotten, misunderstood, or contrived by two male dullards/illiterates. Literacy skills and experience in commerce do not define intelligence. Acuity, wisdom, and devoutness are pervasively illustrated in the Qur'ān as available to both genders through God's grace; that is, such qualities are not gender-specific.

POLYGYNY[5]

The word of God sought to remedy *jahili* abuses of earlier Arabian societies in which polygyny was practiced and all manner of abuse was visited on the captives of war who became slaves. Further, war widows and orphans of the period invariably lost the protection of husbands/fathers. They were thus vulnerable to fraud, theft, abuse, starvation, and sexual predation. In the era of revelation, how were these most vulnerable of the family of humankind to be treated? What standards of care and justice were to be observed by believers if they were now to absorb into their families those of their fallen comrades?

Our views diverge in some respects. Barlas sees 4:1–6 as restricting polygyny to orphans, and then only where a guardian is unable to deal fairly with the orphans outside of marriage (assuming a husband has greater reason to treat his wife's assets properly than he might treat an orphan's for whom he was merely a guardian): a condition of such orphan marriage is that it avoids injustice to the wife. Polygyny, as Barlas sees it, is thus intended solely to ensure social justice for orphaned girls.

In Surah 4, believers are counseled on how they might care for both orphans and, in Finn's view, their mothers.[6]

> Humankind, fear your Lord who created you from a single soul, created your mate, and from these two a multitude of men and women, your kin. Revere God, giver of rights, and wombs, givers of the families of humankind. God watches over your stewardship. (4:1)

> Give orphans what is theirs. Neither switch your impoverished property for their sound assets nor expend their wealth as if it were yours. To do so is certainly a crime. (4:2)

> If you feared you were unable to act justly in respect of the orphans, then marry of the women as seems appropriate, two, three or four. But if you feared you should be unduly partial, marry but one, or her who is rightly yours. This is fitting, that you do not act wrongfully. (4:3)

> With grace provide their dowries for such women as you marry. But if they would remit to you of their dowry, use it contentedly. (4:4)

> Do not impart to the imprudent your wealth, wealth which is God's gift for your family's support. Instead feed and clothe them with it. And address them with words of kindness. (4:5)

> Take the measure of the orphans in your care until they are of marriageable age. Then, if you find they are prudent, grant them their wealth. Forbear the temptation to consume it hastily

> in its entirety before they reach maturity. Whichever guardian among you is rich, he is to refrain from such consumption. If a guardian is poor, he is to consume only what is fair. When you as guardian provide their wealth to them, have your actions witnessed. God witnesses and reckons. (4:6) (emended by Finn)[7]

Patriarchal interpretations read *l-nisai* in *ayah* 4:3 neither as "widows" nor "orphans," but as "other women." Thus they extract the claim that marriage with up to four "other women" is permissible and insist that generalized polygyny is permitted. The patriarchal understanding of 4:3 is illustrated in various translations as "if you fear you will act unjustly toward orphans marry such women as seem good to you," "marry those that please you of other women," "marry women of your choice." However, such readings are problematic. Note first that the word "other" does not appear in the text. Nor does the reading make complete sense. Women who are already protected ("other women" who have families and protectors) are not readily susceptible to "injustice." By contrast, female orphans whose fathers have fallen in battle and the believing mothers of those orphans may be open to victimization, both personal and financial. But no ready explanation suggests how marrying a woman, or several women, who are other than female orphans[8] or the widowed mothers of war orphans would protect the orphans or their widowed mothers. On the other hand, if one were to marry from among "the women" who are war widows, not only would the widow receive protection, but her children would become unlawful to whomever married their mother. The same sort of argument would apply if the ward of female orphans were to marry more than one orphan in his care. Finally, it would indeed be fitting for the guardian of orphans "that he not act wrongfully" (4:3): by marrying a widow or an orphan, he saves himself from damning temptations.

In any case, the *ayat* in question (4:1–6) do not provide a basis for generalized polygyny, even if they permit marriage for up to four wives from among women who might otherwise suffer injustice. Marriage protects both widows and female orphans from predation, and the soul of the spouse from potential wrongdoing. Even then, since a man will almost certainly favor one wife, he is strongly advised to marry her alone. Treating multiple wives equitably is well-nigh impossible (4:129) since God has not given men multiple hearts (33:4).

DIVORCE AND MISREADING 2:228 FOR MALE PRIVILEGE

The Qur'ān acknowledges the possibility of divorce as well as God's preference for harmony and reconciliation: "Peace is better. . . ." (4:128). In pre-Islamic Arabia, divorce was easy, rampant, and almost invariably initiated by men. The revealed Word therefore consistently addresses men by way of offering remedy for the pre-Islamic iniquity men inevitably inflicted on women in divorce. The divorcing couple is enjoined to practice "liberality between themselves" (2:237); men are not to "turn their wives out" of the marital home (65:1), and they are not to take them back in order to injure or take advantage of them (2:231). Men are to provide for wives "on a reasonable scale" (2:241). But at this juncture we must consider one of the Qur'ān's most famous verses because, of all of them, this one is read, indeed favored, by patriarchal apologists as conferring on men a status unmatched by women.

> And women who are being divorced shall wait, without remarrying, three monthly menses. (It is unlawful for them, if they are believers in God and the last day, to conceal what God has created for their wombs.) Their husbands have better right to take them back during this waiting period if they desire reconciliation. Women's rights and responsibilities are like men's, but men's are comparatively greater [*darajatun*]. God is All Powerful and Wise. (2:228 [emended by Finn])[9]

Traditional patriarchal readings of *darajatun* reflect what is almost a palpable glee: "men have a degree over them [in responsibility and authority]" (trans. Sahih International); "men have a degree (of advantage) over them" (trans. Ali); "men have a status above women" (trans. Sarwar); "their men have a degree above them" (trans. Arberry). Do we then have a clear-cut case where the Qur'ān admits what patriarchal apologists profess to know with certainty: that men are favored by God?

Most traditional readings, of which the above are but samples, struggle to identify precisely in what specific sense men's responsibilities and/or authority differ from and exceed those of the wife he is proceeding to divorce. There are heroic efforts:

> Men . . . do not have a waiting period for remarriage for obvious physiological reasons. That is where men have an advantage over women. (trans. Ahmed)[10]

At the risk of disillusioning those who wish to assert male gender superiority based on their reading of *darajatun* in 2:228, we review some obvious points. The Qur'ān offers remedy for *jahili* practices offensive to an all-knowing, just God. Injustices to women were conspicuous among these practices. Just conduct for men who are divorcing women is the subject of 2:228. Characteristically, the Qur'ān begins by wrong-footing the reader. It reminds believers that men who are divorcing their wives deserve justice too: a wife involved in a divorce must observe a waiting period in case she is bearing the husband's child. And, of course, if she's pregnant, she shouldn't try to hide it (however angry or upset she might be). That would be wrong and unlawful. During the waiting period they may wish to reconcile. But there is an obvious question: Who is to initiate the reconciliation?

Evidently, in 2:228, the man has initiated the divorce. (Its opening words refer to *mutalaqatu*, a nominative, feminine plural, passive-voiced gerund meaning "women being divorced.") In this case, it would make little sense for her to approach him: her position (to remain married/not to remain married) is already known to her husband. Since he's the one seeking divorce, it's his responsibility to seek reconciliation if he wishes and to take her back if she is willing. He has the "better right," meaning the greater burden, the clearer responsibility to act. The onus, as Muhammad Asad suggests, is on him.[11] Accordingly, there is no mystery about the "greater degree of responsibility," the "precedence" in rights and responsibilities, that men have in 2:228: it has nothing to do with men having greater authority or loftier status, or being preferred by God or being the breadwinner, and less than nothing to do with men's and women's comparative physiology.

Some commentators link the husband's purported rights as breadwinner for the family to the claim that he has greater right to rescind the petition for divorce. But no mention of a unilateral right to rescind divorce appears in the text of 2:228. Instead, husbands who reconsider divorcing their wives should try for reconciliation if both wish it; that is, the husband's initiation of the divorce locates him, not his wife, as the agent who, having second thoughts, has the obligation to seek reconciliation.

Women and men have equal rights and responsibilities in marriage. However, if men seek to divorce their wives, it's up to them, not the wives, to initiate reconciliation. They are the ones shredding the fabric of their marriage, thus it's incumbent upon them to mend what is torn if the cloth can be repaired. That is a great responsibility indeed. And it is theirs alone, not their wives. So their responsibilities have precedence. They are greater, a "degree" greater than that of wives. Still, a wife must agree to the reconciliation, and, it should be added, if she is feeling shocked, bitter, disappointed, betrayed, or angry and has lost trust, that will be hard enough. Thus understanding 2:228 as pointing to the man as genetically more responsible, as having more rights because he is enjoined by God to be the breadwinner, or as more innately advantaged than women is unsupported by the text. These are evident misreadings.

Further remedies to preexisting injustices surrounding divorce are stated. The Qur'ān denounces the tradition of *zihar* divorce, in which, by publicly assimilating his wife's role to that of his mother, a husband summarily initiates divorce:

> Those who renounce their wives by calling them mothers should know that their wives could never become their mothers. Their mothers are those who have given birth to them. The words that they speak are certainly detestable and sinful. But God is Pardoning and All-forgiving. (58:2 [trans. Sarwar])

A husband is limited in the number of times he may divorce his wife and is forbidden from using divorce to defraud her. She is to remain in the marital home (unless she is openly carrying on an affair), and he is to support her as his means permit (Surah 65:1–12). Kindness and equitable treatment are enjoined whether reconciliation is achieved or alienation persists.

Critical Dilemmas in Interpreting the Qur'ān

DAVID RAEBURN FINN

PATRIARCHAL READINGS of the Qur'ān assert that some (few) verses privilege men. But as *Believing Women* demonstrates, there is little argument that far greater numbers of the Qur'ān's verses insist on the equality of men and women. So these few so-called male-privileging verses are inconsistent with, by far, the greater part of the Word. Nevertheless, traditionalists use them to deny social, political, and sexual equality to women altogether.

So conservative scholars aren't merely asserting that male privilege is inconsistent with the Qur'ān's equality verses. Inconsistency means you say, "I understand the verse so," and I say, "I understand it differently!" With inconsistency we differ over meanings. If we differ on meanings, we tend to discuss the reasons we read something the way we do. Rational discussion, offering reasons, helps to resolve inconsistencies. But if conservative scholars are to hold that the Qur'ān asserts male privilege, they need to rule out those verses asserting equality to show that there's no hope for women's equality in the Qur'ān. According to them, some passages of the Qur'ān "abrogate" others, a fancy word meaning "overturn." On this view, a few verses rule over the many. Conservatives don't merely elevate men over women; they elevate some verses of the Qur'ān over others, verses which they claim, not coincidentally, state that men have an advantage over women, that they may beat their wives, that they can have sex with their wives when and however they wish, and that men, not women, are the heads of households.

A first problem for conservatives is that no verse in the Qur'ān says, "Some verses are more important than others." What then permits patriarchal scholars to claim abrogation of the overwhelming number of so-called equality verses? Do patriarchal scholars ignore the Qur'ān's very clear warning: "What is the matter with you? How could you judge this to be so? Do you have a book from which you study that tells you to do whatever you want?" (68:36–38 [trans. Sarwar]) The Qur'ān enjoins us to read it as a whole. No other book, no second book, is a substitute. And no part or verse of the Holy Book takes precedence over another (even if a given verse may qualify or elaborate on the meaning of another). Moreover, the Qur'ān does not contain contradictions; therefore, the Qur'ān's equality verses cannot be denied by male-privileging ones.

A second problem is that none of the pertinent verses of the Qur'ān support what conservatives say they support. The so-called wife-beating verse (4:34) is a misreading, one shown by Waqas Muhammad to have substituted a modern Arabic meaning ("to beat") for a classical term meaning "to cite" or "report to an authority." Also, no gender advantage is attributed to men in the Qur'ān by verse 2:228, concerning women whom men are divorcing. It merely states what is obvious: if a man initiates divorce but then reconsiders, it's his responsibility to mend fences. The conservative reading of the menses verses (2:222–23) both misunderstands the context in which the verses occur, the when and the why of them, and forces meanings on key words that they will not bear.

The breadwinners verse (also in 4:34) does not install men and only men as the heads of families. Instead it defines a role husbands may play in family life if they satisfy an important proviso, one which equally admits wives as breadwinners (since wives can also support the family with their earnings or wealth).

At this point then, there is no support for the specific claim of abrogation of an egalitarian Qur'ān; that is, there is no support for the contention that male-privileging verses overrule equality verses. However, these are but minor difficulties measured against the chief problems facing conservative scholars, which they create for themselves. We'll look at them one at a time.

First, if some verses of the word of God abrogate others, the inescapable conclusion is that God made mistakes. Do conservative scholars recognize the difficulties with this? How could believers in God's perfection begin to contemplate God making mistakes? We, as human beings, say things we regret and correct them. Does God? We forget or are ignorant of certain facts and speak mistakenly. Can God be forgetful or ignorant of facts? In frustration we speak angrily and falsely. Does God do so? In fact, faith is not consistent with any such conjectures. God is either all-knowing or not. God is either perfection or not. The Qur'ān is either the perfect word of God or not. Believers accept an all-knowing, perfect God and submit to the Word, or they do not. A simpler explanation for what conservative scholars mistake for abrogation, for their reading of some verses as gender-privileging, is that they are the ones who have erred in suggesting that these verses of the Qur'ān abrogate others, and they are the ones who have misunderstood those verses claimed as incontestably privileging men.

The second dilemma for conservative scholars stems from their "second book," that is, the books of received *ahadith* and the character of the Prophet. *Believing Women* frames the dilemma broadly: What are we to make of those *ahadith* attributed to the Prophet which are read by conservatives to support either inconsistency or abrogation? Recall that *ahadith* are deemed to explain difficulties of the Qur'ān. But insofar as explanatory *ahadith* support supposed inconsistencies or abrogations, then conservative scholars must claim the Prophet's support for them. Are we to believe that the bearer of God's word recognized but failed to proclaim divine contradictions? Did this most admirable of men, honest, alert and intelligent, chosen by God, forget, fail to pay attention, or fail to understand certain revelations? Is it not simpler to question conservative scholars' reliance on such *ahadith*? What evidence could convince believers to accept that conservative scholars understand the Qur'ān perfectly, but the Prophet, who proclaimed the word of God, did not? No verse of the Qur'ān concedes that its revelations may contain errors or omissions. If received narrations of the Prophet's practice, the *ahadith*, are used to support claims of internal inconsistency or abrogation in the Qur'ān, then the *ahadith* must be suspected. Of course, for those who claim that their knowledge of the Prophet's life and his understanding of the Word is greater than the Prophet's, their understanding too must be suspected.

MODERN CRITICS

Those who believe that some verses of the Qur'ān are incontestably male privileging may seek to avoid these difficulties. They may grant that the Qur'ān is internally consistent, so non-abrogated. What seem to be contradictions arise because the male-privileging verses merely acknowledge established rights of the revelatory period, rights different from those of the modern era. This amounts to the claim that equality and justice within the revelatory era may have been seen differently from what modern readers take them to be. Such rights, on this view, included male status as breadwinners and gender-based male sexual privilege founded on the Qur'ān's estimate of the male gender's natural superiority within an otherwise equal community of believers.[1] Women's equality in the revelatory era consisted in their being spiritual equals, not social, political, or sexual equals.

So, on this view, God's word is infallible, but the Word doesn't invariably support an anti-patriarchal, anti-misogynistic, and egalitarian vision of liberating *tafsir*. The egalitarian Qur'ān nonetheless privileges men. The evidence offered in such readings is, first, that the Qur'ān addresses men, not women, about sex and marriage. Moreover, men are addressed as agents, while women are ignored except to be noted as passive objects available to men's agency. On this view, the Qur'ān countenances a community of equal believers in which gender meritocracy naturally favors men. It is a community of equal souls. But living male bearers of souls have more rights on this earth than women bearers of souls.

Let's take apart this view piece by piece. What if it were true that the Qur'ān more often than not addresses men rather than women on matters of marriage and sexuality? What could explain this?

As Asma Barlas has argued, the facts are that the Qur'ān ordained remedies for injustices inflicted upon those victimized in *jahili* societies. The fact that the Qur'ān ordained such remedies explains precisely why the text addresses men more than women (or, to use the scholarly term, why the Qur'ān's language is androcentric). The Qur'ān recalls, for an errant humanity, human perfection. If its message is preponderantly addressed to men, it is because the conduct of men was conspicuous in its injustices toward women. It was not as though women were inflicting injustices on men. Women were the victims of injustices, so the appropriate audience requiring correction would have been their oppressors.

Here it's interesting to note the first occasion in which God addresses the issue of the Qur'ān's androcentricity. Umm Salama, a wife of the Prophet, asks why men are mentioned in the Qur'ān when women are not. God's response (33:35) enumerates the virtues expected of both men and women, as if to explain that human perfection is no different between the sexes. Men are specifically and predominately addressed because they are perpetrators of injustices against women. Women need look no further than the Qur'ān's counsels of perfection to see that their perfection is no different from that of men.

Those who support a male-privileging Qur'ān rely on two scant observations. The first is that the Qur'ān predominantly addresses men in connection with marriage and sexuality. Insofar as this observation is based on facts, the facts are easily explained and do not support male-privileging. Rather, they acknowledge in the immediate post-*jahili* world that men's past injustices now face a liberating revelation.

The second observation is that an egalitarian Qur'ān must be a misreading. The evidence for this bald claim lies in the undraped assertions that the Word reveals men to be superior to women because some verses are incontrovertibly male-privileging, incontrovertible in that by trying to find different meanings, we reach a semantic dead end. Simply put, patriarchal scholars claim that no one can provide for these verses a sense different from those that they have attributed to them.

But liberating readings of each of the verses central to patriarchal readings of the Qur'ān reveal the claim of a semantic dead end as without merit. The notion that no other sense can be read from the verses in question is simply eyewash. Even if egalitarian readings were subject to objections that they are as flawed as patriarchal ones, traditional scholars must claim that no other reading is conceivable, now or ever.

Let's review one of the so-called male-privileging verses favored by traditional apologists. We'll concede certain patriarchal semantic contentions in order to show that patriarchal readings of the Qur'ān's menses verses (2:222–23) can't be sustained even on their own terms.

Patriarchal understanding of a key phrase in 2:223 includes serious confusions. The crucial Arabic phrase is *fatu harth akum anna shi'tum*, in which *fatu* is the second-person imperative of the verb "to approach." Patriarchal readings suggest the phrase as a whole has the sense "approach [literally, 'come to'] your tilth [*harth akum*] when or how you will" (trans. Ali). Because the imperative is used, patriarchal readings find that the verse prescribes or enjoins "coming to" one's wife. Use of the imperative is then cited as a command that the wife must submit to sex with her husband. This is a clear mistake. Even if *fatu* were an unvarnished command (it isn't), it would command merely that the husband approach or come to his wife. If a driving instructor asks his pupil to approach the car ahead, the pupil has not been instructed to collide with the vehicle ahead. Nor has the driver of the lead vehicle been commanded to permit the collision. Even if *fatu* were to command (and it does not), a wife is not commanded to assent.

In fact, the chief error in such a reading is that the imperative in Arabic, as in English, has several uses, and the use here is evidently permissive. By comparison, consider the child who wishes to go out but must complete his chores first.

Child: "When can I go out?"
Father/Mother: "Go out when you finish your chores."

The imperative here grants the permission asked for. It doesn't command that the child go out. There would be no point to doing so: the child has already asked whether he might go out. We noted earlier that believers, including the Prophet's Companions, were familiar with the Jewish tradition that countenanced a total of fourteen days during which a wife's menses and its aftermath left her impure, preventing sexual contact. In 2:222–23 the question when normal sexual relations might resume in relation to menses is answered for the newly revealed monotheism. A divine command ("Commence sex after menses!") can no more be read into 2:222–23 than a parent's command ("Go out after your chores!") can be read into a reply to the son who has asked permission to go out.

The second clear confusion, unsupported by the text, lies in reading the Arabic *anna* (see Ali) to mean "when or how." Translations of *anna* from the Arabic suggest it plays precisely the role of the English "as." But "as" meaning "how" depends on context.[2] The immediately preceding verse, 2:222, provides the context. It shows that 2:223 responds to questions. Those questions are not about the different sexual acts one might practice with one's wife; they are not questions about whether one may "come to" one's wife in this manner, in that manner, and so on. Rather, as Barlas has noted, they concern when one may approach a wife in the time surrounding her menses: all of the conditions specified for approaching her are temporal (not for the seven days of her menses, then after her ablutions). So permission is granted as to when one may come to one's wife, not as to how one may approach her.

Finally, even if one accepts patriarchal scholars' attempts to deny women's sexual agency in their readings of 2:222–23, those readings confuse misogynistic contempt for reality. *Believing Women* notes that the sense ascribed by traditionalists to the metaphorical *harth* of "tilth" or "field" doesn't bear scrutiny for the reasons given in chapter 6. But for present purposes, let's allow it.

"Tilth" can refer to soil yet to be cultivated, but also to soil already prepared, already cultivated, ready for seeding. Are men to "come to" their wives to seed them? Is this the sense in which they are to cultivate their tilth? If so, then 2:223 cannot grant men permission to come to their wives "however" they wish because some sexual acts are inconsistent with seeding. Still, the question remains: Are men permitted to come to their wives to seed them? Let's agree that they are. But what they are to seed, their tilth, is a soil prepared to be seeded, so an already cultivated soil, one sufficiently enriched by some practice or effort to be fertile. How has it been prepared for seeding?

The answer clearly provided in the verse is that the wife has experienced monthly menses and performed ritual bathing. Thus, it is her actions that prepare for sexual activity. Her husband has no role in cultivation. She is the sole active participant. If men are privileged in this context, it is solely by grace of their wives' agency, not of a text allegedly enjoining male sexual predation.

Misogynistic traditions in misreading the Qur'ān's 2:222–23 fix on degrading women by associating their role with that of a passive soil which their men are invited to act upon. Misogynist traditionalists have misread these verses even on their own terms. The *ayat* instead grant leave for men to seek intimacy from their wives after post-menses purification. (Similar leave is granted after fast is broken during Ramadan, as Barlas notes.) No Qur'ānic direction expresses, no *ayah* ordains that men should be the only active participants in determining anything about sexual conduct within marriage; what 2:222–23 does show is that it is the wife who is responsible for preparing for and permitting sex. The strictly misogynistic traditionalist reading of 2:223 shows only that men have a singular role in which they are the active participants, that of seeding. Their activity in this respect is anatomical and offers no evidence of authority, privilege, or superior status.

To sum up: male control of marital intimacy is neither ordained nor implied in 2:223. If "tilth" is equivalent to "what they cultivate," then several other observations are pertinent. "Tilth" is what is prepared for cultivation, and the husband evidently plays no active role in that process. It's the wife who, through presumably self-conscious ritual bathing, prepares herself for his approach. No part of 2:223 indicates that his "approach" entails a man's right to sexual intimacy without regard to his wife's consent.

Shrewd egalitarian readers may object to the claim that the husband plays no active role in preparing the "cultivation." Their observation would be accurate. After all, the Qur'ān's pervasively egalitarian verses describe and authorize a husband's role, albeit an indirect one, as a cultivar. His marital role directly and seamlessly supports a liberating Qur'ān and is inconsistent with the misogynist interpretation of verses such as 2:222–23. If, as the Qur'ān repeatedly describes in the mutuality of marriage, a husband has cared for his wife, has shown gentle kindness and generosity, his love and respect may have encouraged her self-aware activities of "tilling," that is, her ritual bathing.

Notice that if this is how the husband's contribution to the cultivation of "his tilth" is conceived, it is utterly mutual, reciprocated by her indication (her ritual bathing) that she welcomes his intimacy. Equally, if this is the husband's contribution, it conflicts with male-privileging in sexuality in that it marks only the shared nurturing of mutual marital affection. Not incidentally, such an explanation also makes far greater sense of understanding *harth* as a reference not to soil found in gardens and available for seeding, but to the "garden" of intimacy itself in which mutual cultivation and responsiveness are found and nourished (see chapter 6). "Garden" is an appropriate metaphor in the English language for a prepared soil which both nourishes those who tend it and is nourished by them. Far from mutuality and love being disconnected from sexual conduct, the liberating reading of 2:222–23 provides a flawless conjoining of affectionate intimacy with sexuality.

Perhaps the Qur'ān is wiser than many of its traditionalist readers in recognizing that in the complexity of sexuality, including the seeking of intimacy, active participation may sometimes take the path of selecting an apparent passivity, a path that may be chosen by either partner. Further, within the depth of intimacy it is difficult to imagine that conduct conditioned by mutuality, respect, and kindness would eliminate the active participation of either partner, even when active participation consists of some degree of passivity. Only a regrettable misogynistic tunnel vision might confuse a woman's welcome gesture of acceptance with an ordained right to insist that she accept.

So traditionalists claim in such verses as 2:222–23 that a semantic dead end is reached: no reading different from a gender-favoring one can be found. It's a grandly empty claim. If 2:222–23 did, in fact, instruct husbands to ignore all verses enjoining mutual respect, equal rights to *sukun* (serenity), and kindness in intimate conduct between marital partners, some solid evidence of male privilege might be evident. A diagnosis of men's primacy in 2:222–23 would be supported if the Qur'ān anywhere indicated that believing wives were incapable of understanding the ritual role of post-menstrual bathing, if they were instructed in 2:222–23 invariably to assent to their husband's imprecations, or, alternatively, were genetically incapable of myriad responses and gestures available through God's grace implying hesitation, assent, warmth, denial, or enthusiasm in response to a husband's seeking of intimacy. It is, regrettably, characteristic of a hopelessly senseless misogyny that it might insist that permission to seek intimacy with one's wife post-menses should be coupled with an estimate of her role that obliterates her capacity for understanding, affection, and human agency.

The traditionalists' hope was that the Qur'ān's allegedly rock-solid male-privileging verses marked a concept of social equality fitting the revelatory era of proclamation. Men were privileged in family and society because of men's Qur'ān-ordained superiority. In other respects, men and women enjoyed equal status in God's eyes. The allegedly male-privileging verses marked that superiority: God saw equality as compatible with a gender-based pecking order specifically for the era of revelation. For traditionalists, current attempts to find a liberating Qur'ān are therefore attempts to impose, improperly, modern concepts of justice and equality on the earlier era.

But this charge relies on the existence in the Qur'ān of rock-solid verses ordaining men's superiority, because if God did not ordain men's superiority in the proclaimed Word, then the Qur'ān's equality and justice are our own and always have been. In each case we have examined, allegedly rock-solid gender-favoring verses appear to have been misunderstood and misread by traditionalists. In some cases, as in 2:222–23, traditionalist readings are thoroughly confused, incoherent on their own terms. To conclude, since the Qur'ān does not in fact contain male-privileging verses, let alone rock-solid ones, the claim that it ordains men's superiority is without merit. God's word is, instead, egalitarian.

That supposedly male-privileging *ayat* are indicative of a sense of justice and equality peculiar to the seventh century is belied both by the Qur'ān and revelatory-period justice. Consider the believing husband of 4:34 who beats his disaffected wife for refusing reconciliation. Recognition that such conduct constituted an injustice is reflected in Islam's earliest history: such a beating, from the beginning, provided grounds for a wife to initiate divorce. In respect of *qiwamah* (breadwinner status), no modern theory of equality is needed to show that women of the era of revelation could be, and were, breadwinners for their families. All contemporary revelatory Companions and believers knew that Hazrat Khadija was a conspicuous example of a woman satisfying the definition of a breadwinner offered in 4:34. Every seventh-century widow who supported her family was a contemporary counter-example to the traditionalist misreading of *qiwamah* as an exclusively male role. Further, no peculiarly modern notion of inequality is applied in seeing the traditionalist (mis)reading of women as men's metaphorical *harth* to mean "tilth," where this includes a further confusion implying a wife's availability for "seeding" without regard to her consent and, indeed, against her will. Kind and gentle conduct between husband and wife is specifically enjoined in the revelatory Qur'ān, a prescription which from the beginning undermines traditional understandings taken from 2:222–23. Islam's history, which saw wife-beating as a ground for divorce, women breadwinners, and reciprocal nurturing of marital partners, belies the notion that the justice and equality of the seventh century were culturally alienated from a modern sense of justice and equality. The Qur'ān's enjoining of mutual respect, tenderness, and sexual reciprocity within marriage pointedly argues against a misreading of *harth* as suggesting women are passive, inertly fertile receptacles for male seeding. Instead these instructions promote a recognizably modern sexual equality. Thus the idea that egalitarian *tafsir* represents an inauthentic Islam, a surreptitious foisting of modern and alien Western concepts of equality and justice upon Islam, is denied both by Islam's history and the Qur'ān itself.

AFTERWORD

Converging Themes

DAVID RAEBURN FINN

The Qur'ān, of which I am a student rather than scholar, offers to humanity remedies for injustices founded on deprivations and iniquities. It surfaced in a *jahili* era in which the miseries of an afflicted class remained opaque, invisible to society's ascendant and entitled class, that is, to men. The man who oversaw the birth of the Word was the Prophet.

My education, in Canada and the UK, was as a philosopher. By the time of my doctoral studies in Great Britain, the religious concerns of philosophers such as Aquinas, Abelard, Avicenna, Averroes, Gazzali, and Maimonides had been, as contemporary thought would have it, washed away by a robust secularism waving a banner of common sense. Religious issues, in any case only rarely and momentarily including reference to Islam, largely disappeared from British philosophy of the period. Where notable Christians in Great Britain such as Elizabeth Anscombe and C. S. Lewis professed religious beliefs, such beliefs were regularly conceded to be personal quirks, which is to say quaint and unfortunate adornments viewed rather in the manner of tolerable afflictions. If I were to make Islam's acquaintance, it would have to be by wandering into it, not direct immersion.

Several events in life outside academia conspired to invite my interest in Islam. On the one hand, I'd met, admired, and learned from a comparatively uneducated refugee who proved to be a mosque counselor, a national coordinator for university student placements, and a business whiz. On the other, I witnessed the disintegration of a marriage of friends, both believers, largely because the husband insisted on mysterious (to me) rights apparently prescribed by his faith and not available to his believing wife. Coincidentally I'd begun writing a novel about a Pukhtun widow victimized in war. For background I'd consulted with a Cambridge anthropologist, a Pukhtun woman herself and the daughter of a distinguished scholar of Islam based in the United States. The anthropologist's book took issue with an American counterpart whose writings, among other things, had found Islam guilty of making Pukhtun women "miserable and powerless." The heroine in my novel was anything but miserable and powerless. In any case, my instincts were that faulting Islam was one ethnocentricity too many.

I conferred with more Pukhtuns online. They included an impressive blogger working on a PhD at the University of Texas and an equally impressive Canadian father of four who is multilingual, a proud Pukhtun familiar with current world events, and deeply devout. My background reading now included several biographies of the Prophet, including Ibn Ishaq's original one. None of the biographies convincingly addressed an issue about which I was increasingly curious, an issue raised by a character in my novel: What was it that made the character of the Prophet so compelling for his biographers and for the Muslims I'd met? How could I illustrate this in my tale? I fixed on his first wife, Khadija. I wanted to see him through her eyes: Who would know a man better than the first believer, a sophisticated and mature woman who had been so strongly drawn to him that she proposed their marriage soon after meeting him? So it was that I began looking for information about Khadija, which led me to place a call to someone I'd never met. My hopes had been stirred by a book title, *"Believing Women" in Islam* (Austin: University of Texas Press, 2002), written by Asma Barlas. If she had written about believing women, surely she had touched on Khadija, mother of believers. Alas, Professor Barlas dashed my soaring hopes: Khadija wasn't mentioned in *"Believing Women."* Hers was a treatise hoping to rescue the Islam she believed the Qur'ān revealed from one corrupted by conservative patriarchal readings. I noted her book, ordered and read it. It would be an understatement to say I was impressed. I wanted to contact her immediately to say so. Instead, though it often occurred to me to contact her, it took almost three years to do it. In the meantime I'd had more time with my novel.

I realized that *"Believing Women"* bore on a critical issue of a kind faced by my novel's heroine, who is victimized and dishonored. Her life is put at risk not because of her actions, but because of a cultural priority afforded to men's honor. What could give believing men a sense that their honor might mean the death of a woman victimized by other men?

In the several biographies I'd read of the Prophet, I was unable to locate his claim to greater rights than those of his wives or of any women. I found no reference to his sense that he should be afforded greater respect, that his pride took precedence over that of others, that he possessed greater intellectual capacity than women, a greater love of truth, a greater capacity for the skills of life. My impression, perhaps romanticized, was that he loved women deeply, treasuring both their intimacy and company, and valuing their counsel and conversation. With all that, he was remarkably humble yet, when necessary, extraordinarily courageous. He seemed exceptional in other ways: generous almost to a fault, great hearted, and devoid of malice. Some stories about him stood out: Ibn Ishaq's story of Tufayl of the Bani Daws illustrates the Prophet's kindness; that of Al Nuayman ibn Amr reveals the Prophet's fulsome and generous sense of humor.

In *"Believing Women,"* Professor Barlas describes an Islam that a man such as the Prophet would have reveled in bringing to humanity, an Islam providing remedy to the dispossessed and oppressed of *jahili* society. She undertook the project courteously, suggesting that readings of the Qur'ān endorsing the primacy of men were but one interpretative possibility. With careful research, acknowledging the many scholars who came before her, Barlas suggested that an egalitarian reading of the Qur'ān is equally possible and, for myriad reasons, more plausible.

"*Believing Women*" articulates a different realm in understanding Islam that I had begun to sense without defining. I found it brilliant, riveting, and convincing. It defined and spoke for a resolution of a central conflict in Islam: a male elite claiming unique and exclusive expertise in the interpretation of the Qur'ān's meaning. Barlas provides a rational account not only of the perversities of the process grounding the claim for interpretative exclusivity, but also a compelling basis for disputing interpretations of the Qur'ān issuing from that self-blessed authority. She argues that rereading the Qur'ān for equality is both possible and encouraged by the Word itself. Her writing provided a scaffold of support for those courageous rebels within Muslim jurisdictions where resurgent *jahili* practices enforce the rights and privileges of men at the expense of crushing those for women.

"*Believing Women*" exemplifies an understanding of Islam against which the extraordinary humanity of its first believer is illuminated. It provides an understanding that denies Qur'ānic support for injustices against women and gender-based male primacy within households, societies, and legal jurisdictions. Yet, in one respect, I suspected Barlas's brilliant work didn't accomplish what it could and should.

I had to contact her, but was intimidated. How could I acknowledge her scholarship, its importance and wisdom, yet suggest that needed work had not been done? Even more daunting, I wished to suggest that I, a philosopher and mere student of Islam, might propose how she might further her work, a proposal in which I would play a role. At this point, you should realize that we had no real acquaintance, no knowledge of one another.

My terror grew: though it is utterly against my instincts to tread into the minefield of generalization, it is so well known as to go without saying that academics share many characteristics with crocodiles, being difficult, tendentious, protective of their territory, argumentative, sensitive even to the scent of criticism. (As to stories that the pet dogs of some academics instinctively run to hide under the bed, tails between their legs, when their masters or mistresses come home from work, I discounted them completely.) Even more importantly, I worried that at a personal level she might find, like so many of my overly judgmental friends, that my extended soliloquies needed occasional interruption if only to permit the appearance of polite conversation. Worse yet, might she take my praise for *"Believing Women"* as servile pandering in the interest of self-promotion?

My proposal was to produce a condensed *"Believing Women,"* in simpler prose, absent as many scholarly references and technical terms as possible while retaining fundamental messages. I believed its message, Asma Barlas's message, should be made available to the widest possible audience. My conviction is that many believing men and women of goodwill remain largely predisposed to accept without question, study, or critical inquiry the deeply flawed patriarchal dictums purported to originate in the Qur'ān. Perhaps, just perhaps, understanding the process by which patriarchal traditionalists have come to exercise so much authority in today's Islam, together with seeing a plainspoken revised reading of some of the most controversial of the Qur'ān's verses, might stimulate believers' critical interrogation of patriarchal dogma.

Would Professor Barlas view the proposal as an academic folly, a degradation of her scholarship?

In the end, as you see, I did contact her, and we agreed to work together, she as the editor who has saved her student from many errors while denying with kindness his too frequent spontaneous eruptions of misplaced humor. I've learned from her wisdom and patience. I am grateful for her generosity and honored to have helped.

NOTES

CHAPTER 5

1. Translation is Ali's except "No, you are simply people" has been substituted for Ali's "No, you are simply men."

2. Finn: "Some considerable evidence suggests 'Ayesha (Aisha), said by some to be nine years at the consummation of her marriage to the Prophet, was instead a young woman." See online: http://www.discoveringislam.org/aisha_age.htm.

3. Khadija, though a widow, was neither impoverished nor in any financial need.

CHAPTER 6

1. Translation is Ali's except "O humankind" has been substituted for Ali's "O mankind."

2. Finn: "Here Ali's 'tranquility' [*sukun*] has been replaced by 'serenity' in the interest of a more felicitous English. After all, 30.21 of the Qur'ān addresses love, that is, marital intimacy. It isn't speaking of soothing glasses of warm milk (said to be calming)."

3. Ali's "believing men" has been replaced by "believers."

4. Finn has varied Ali's English translation of two key Arabic metaphorical phrases for reasons he makes explicit in subsequent paragraphs.

CHAPTER 7

1. Muhammad, *Wife Beating in Islam?*.

2. Finn: "More felicitously: '. . . so righteous women are devout, guarding unseen what God has guarded. . . . as for those women whose alienation you fear, then counsel them.'"

3. Finn: "I find certain phrases in Waqas Muhammad's translations of these *ayah* unclear. I've reworded each verse in an attempt to clarify it for myself while retaining the sense I take from it."

4. Pickthall's translation (*The Meaning of The Glorious Koran* [1936]) begins: "Then if they obey you. . . ." But no commands that the wife could obey follow: rather, the husband is instructed to advise/counsel the recalcitrant wife and then abandon her bed, actions which might elicit a(n) (un)favorable response, rather than *obedience*.

5. *Polygyny* refers to the practice of having many wives or many women as mates; its opposite is *polyandry*, having many men as mates. Each is a form of polygamy (plural marriage or plural union).

6. See Barlas, *"Believing Women" in Islam* (2002), 189–192. Finn notes that Surah 4 is thought to have been revealed subsequent to the Battle of Uhud, in which believers lost seventy men. He therefore reads 4:1–6 to address believers on issues of treating justly the martyred believers' surviving widows (the "women" referred to in 4:3), their children, and their property, including slaves. Muhammad Sarwar reads: "With respect to marrying widows if you are afraid of not being able to maintain justice with her children. . . ." (4:3).

7. Finn: "The wording of these verses (4:1–6) was distilled from noble if disparate English translations, none of which seemed to offer consistently clear or concise English."

8. Barlas's reading of the verse is that it restricts and limits polygyny to the orphans themselves and does not extend to their mothers, much less to other women.

9. Finn: "Wording taken from sundry English translations."

10. See Shabbir Ahmed, *The Qur'ān As It Explains Itself* (PDF), QXPvi, 2015, http://www.ourbeacon.com/wordpress/?page_id=21.

11. Asad, *The Message of the Qur'ān* (Gibraltar: Dar al-Andalus, 1980).

CHAPTER 8

1. See also Aysha A. Hidayatullah, *Feminist Edges of the Qur'ān* (Oxford: Oxford University Press, 2014); and Kecia Ali, *Sexual Ethics and Islam* (Oxford: Oxford University Press, 2006).

2. "As" meaning "how," like "as" meaning "when," takes its meaning from context. For example, if a wife were to ask, "How should I cook it?" the husband might reply, "Fry, steam, or bake it, as [= how] you wish." But if guests are coming at 8 p.m., and the wife delays cooking until the next morning's breakfast, their guests might decide to leave early, leaving the couple's reputation as hosts dashed. "As" means "how" in this context, and the wife has misunderstood its use (possibly deliberately) to imply that she can cook dinner *both how* and *when* she pleases.

SELECT BIBLIOGRAPHY

Ali, Kecia. *Sexual Ethics and Islam: Feminist Reflections on Qur'ān, Hadith, and Jurisprudence*. Oxford: Oneworld, 2006.

Ali, Yusuf. *The Holy Qur'ān: Translation and Commentary*. 1934. Reprint, Birmingham, UK: Islamic Vision, 2001.

Alislami Almunatada Trust. *The Qur'ān: Arabic Text with Corresponding English Meanings*. Sahih International. London, UK: Abdul Qasim, 1997.

al-Tabari, Muhammad. *The Commentary on the Quran*. Translated by J. Cooper. Oxford: Oxford University Press, 1987.

Arberry, Arthur John. *The Koran Interpreted: A Translation*. 1955. Reprint, New York: Touchstone, 1996

Asad, Muhammad. *The Message of the Qur'ān*. Gibraltar: Dar al-Andalus, 1980.

Barlas, Asma. *"Believing Women" in Islam: Unreading Patriarchal Interpretations of the Qur'ān*. Austin: University of Texas Press, 2002.

Hidayatullah, Aysha A. *Feminist Edges of the Qur'ān*. New York: Oxford University Press, 2014.

Muhammad, Waqas. *Wife Beating in Islam? The Qur'ān Strikes Back!* Self-published, Amazon Digital Services, 2011. Kindle and www.Quran434.com.

Pickthall, Mohammed Marmaduke. *The Meaning of the Glorious Koran*. 1930. Reprint, New York: Plume, 1997.

Sarwar, Muhammad. *The Holy Qur'ān: Arabic Text and English Translation*. New York: Islamic Seminary, 1981.

Wadud, Amina. *Qur'ān and Woman: Rereading the Sacred Text from a Woman's Perspective*. 2nd ed. Oxford: Oxford University Press, 1999.

INDEX